Product
Life Cycles and
Product
Management

Recent Titles from Quorum Books

Product Life Cycles and Product Management

Sak Onkvisit
&
John J. Shaw

Q

QUORUM BOOKS

New York • Westport, Connecticut • London

Library of Congress Cataloging-in-Publication Data

Onkvisit, Sak.
  Product life cycles and product management.

  Includes index.
  1. Product life cycle.   2. Product management.
I. Shaw, John J.   II. Title.
HF5415.155.055   1989   658.5'038   88-26509
ISBN 0-89930-319-6 (lib. bdg. : alk. paper)

British Library Cataloguing in Publication Data is available.

Library of Congress Catalog Card Number: 88-26509
ISBN: 0-89930-319-6

First published in 1989 by Quorum Books

Greenwood Press, Inc.
88 Post Road West, Westport, Connecticut 06881

Printed in the United States of America

The paper used in this book complies with the Permanent Paper Standard issued by the National Information Standards Organization (Z39.48-1984).

10 9 8 7 6 5 4 3 2 1

To my family (S.O.)
and
Ann, Jonathan, and Rebecca (J.S.)

Contents

Preface

This book should be of interest to product/brand managers, corporate planners, entrepreneurs, academics, and general readers interested in marketing and management. The book covers many topics only alluded to in similar works. It thus provides a complete and systematic treatment of the varying perspectives and dimensions of product management that would otherwise be available only by consulting numerous different sources.

The book is also suitable as a text for courses in "product management" and "marketing management." The importance of "product management" is underscored by an increasing number of colleges and universities that offer courses dealing specifically with "product."

There are very few professional books in this area. Academic books in the area of marketing management and principles of marketing, in contrast, tend to cover this subject briefly as only one of the many topics or chapters. We thus believe that there is a need as well as a demand for a book devoted entirely to the treatment of this important topic.

At one end are guidebooks or handbooks which provide checklists and simply discuss steps involved in the introduction and management of a product. This is a mechanical approach which overlooks the dynamics in the marketplace. These books may also use a particular case study as the main theme. The problem is that each situation then becomes a unique phenomenon since there is no explicit attempt to identify common problems, characteristics, and guidelines which apply across a variety of products. Without a theoretical framework, seasoned professionals themselves may simply know what they have to do while only vaguely understanding the rationale behind their decisions.

At another end, there are academic books that cover scholarly works based on the empirical and conceptual aspects. The problem is that the treatment of the managerial strategies are at best implicit and brief. Management thus finds it difficult to ascertain the usefulness and relevance of the concepts and theories.

This book attempts to bridge the gap between the two approaches by providing a proper balance. Instead of merely citing isolated business incidents, it seeks to provide a theoretical foundation for the study and understanding of the diverse management practices. Also, instead of describing marketing concepts in abstract terms, the book emphasizes a pragmatic approach. The major thrust of this book is to emphasize the integration of theories, applications, and managerial implications. The balance between actual practices and scholarly materials should provide a meaningful framework for strategic decisions.

PART I

FRAMEWORK FOR PRODUCT PLANNING

1

Basic Product Decisions

PRODUCT DEFINITION

A worthy marketer understands the importance of starting with a definition of the product. Yet, despite this fundamental premise, many companies fail to define their products properly. Conventionally and conveniently, a product is often—much too often—defined only in terms of its physical attributes (e.g., length, width, color, weight, and materials used). This narrow definition is shortsighted and misleading because consumers are usually less interested in these physical characteristics and more in the functions and benefits derived from or associated with such physical materials. A marketer must thus regard his product in an open-minded and broad context.

Consumers buy ice cream not because of the physical ingredients but because they expect much more. As explained by Irvin Robbins of Baskin-Robbins, "We don't sell ice cream; we sell fun." Baskin-Robbins's

Exhibit 1.1
A Total Product

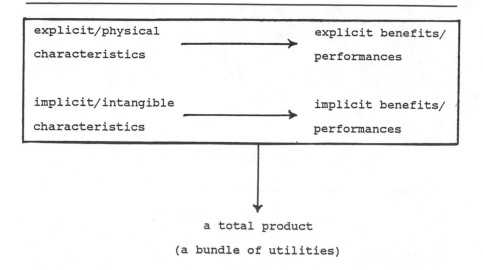

variety of ice cream flavors is a reflection of this statement. Among the flavors offered are Nutcracker Sweet, Jack Lemmon, Hold that Lime, and Here Comes the Fudge. Based on a similar philosophy is Chipwich's marketing practice of requiring its vendors to wear safari suits and pith helmets. Its rival, Dolly Madison, which markets Chip 'n' Chip, sells "fun" by opting for baseball style uniforms—gold and white pinstripe suits and baseball-like caps.

Essentially, a product contains both explicit and implicit characteristics (see Exhibit 1.1). These characteristics in turn provide explicit and implicit benefits (or performances). The product's explicit characteristics are very evident since they deal with the product's physical attributes. As such, these characteristics provide the conventional but flawed definition of a product. The physical configuration of the product makes the explicit performance possible. A TV set, with its push buttons, cabinet, screen, and other physical components, makes it possible for an owner to turn the set off and on for viewing. From a legal standpoint, these physical components are the product's expressed and/or implied warranty with regard to the suitability of the merchandise for consumption as intended. Whenever a product is sold, it is sold with the understanding that it must be capable of performing what it was designed and intended to do (i.e., its primary, basic function[s]). A radio, for example, must give sound, and a car must be capable of being driven.

A product, however, also possesses implicit characteristics which are for the most part intangible. These implicit characteristics, although less obvious and often overlooked, can be just as, if not more, important than their tangible counterparts. Such implicit attributes may include brand name, delivery, installation, repair, and reliability. To put it another way, these attributes are often derived from the other three Ps of marketing—place (distribution), promotion, and pricing. These implicit attributes offer implicit performance in the sense that they provide certain rewards that are associated with some brands but not with others. While all cars offer the same basic and obvious benefit (i.e., transportation), some offer a greater number of implicit benefits. A Cadillac is certainly different from a Yugo or a Hyundai in terms of implicit performance (e.g., prestige). Sony, likewise, consciously emphasizes the brand's implicit aspects by proclaiming "It's a Sony."

It can be said that the physical configuration and explicit performance are the seller's concern while the psychological attributes and implicit performance represent the buyer's viewpoint of the product. Because of consumers' concern with implicit performance, a manufacturer must look beyond the product's physical configuration. Consumers buy a product not just for what it does but also for what it means. In other words, consumers often base their purchase of products on symbolic representations within those products such as fashion, value, status, prestige, and so forth.

The importance of a product's implicit performance was clearly shown in the case of the Rolls-Royce automobile. Rolls-Royce, between 1919 and 1931, had a U.S. manufacturing plant in Springfield (Massachusetts). After producing only 1,240 cars there, the company decided to close the plant because American millionaires felt that the Rolls-Royce cars built there were not authentic.

The mystique of the Rolls-Royce was explained by the company's chief executive: "Our competition is yachts, private aircraft, second and third homes. It's not competition with another automobile but competition with people's money." The point was echoed by the company's sales and marketing director: "We are not selling transportation. You buy a Rolls-Royce because you don't need it. You buy it because it is exclusive, different, and because of its longevity."

The marketing function involves the integration and coordination of all of the mentioned product components (i.e., tangible and intangible attributes and explicit and implicit benefits). If liquor is taken as an example, physically, the product is a bottle which contains alcohol and its explicit function is to intoxicate the drinker. But as explained by Edgar Bronfman of Seagram, "One can get just as drunk drinking cheap stuff." As a result, what Seagram is really selling is the implicit aspect—the glamor and prestige that is found in a bottle of Seagram.

Theodore Levitt has expressed that a product has four elements which need to be distinguished: generic product, expected product, augmented product, and potential product.[1] A *generic* product is merely the physical item or "bare bones" service. In contrast, an *expected* product offers more value than a generic product because it includes certain minimum features (i.e., customers' minimum purchase requirements such as delivery, terms of sale, and supporting advice). An *augmented* product goes a step farther since it includes additional features to enhance the product's attractiveness. This is the case which the supplier, through such means as a better quality control, is able to exceed his customer's expectations. And finally, a *potential* product is one which radically changes the product and market from what the product presently is to what it has the potential of becoming. This kind of product includes things which could be done to attract new customers (e.g., technical changes or new technological applications).

It can be seen that a generic product is primarily preoccupied with the physical configuration and explicit performance. Strategic market advantage, however, can only be achieved by endowing the product with greater benefits. That is, whenever possible, a generic product must be transformed into a potential product (or at least something in between—either an expected product or an augmented product). A narrow definition of a product must be replaced by a broader definition. Federal Express's view of mail service is an example of a potential product. Its redefinition of this service has forced the U.S. Postal Service to reconsider its service mix and to offer its own overnight delivery service. Ironically, the overnight letter and package business is itself being threatened by facsimile machines and electronic mail.

It must be pointed out that, just like its tangible counterpart, a service must be broadly defined as well. One reason for the success of Club Med is its marketing philosophy and product definition. Its goal is to give customers the best vacation for their precious and irreplaceable time. As explained by the company, "we at Club Med are marketing a total leisure experience . . . as opposed to marketing and selling a hotel room, or a specific destination."

PRODUCT AS A BUNDLE OF UTILITIES

Economists have long defined a product as a bundle of utilities (satisfactions). At first glance, the definition seems too abstract to be of any use to a marketer. A closer examination, however, reveals that the definition captures the essence of the product concept remarkably well. Although all products provide some kind of satisfaction, successful products are those which offer a better "bundle" of benefits. The phenomenal success of Merrill Lynch's Cash Management Account (CMA) is due to its bundling strategy. At the time, CMA was a highly innovative product which combined money market funds, a checking account, and Visa debit card into a single product.

By viewing a product as a bundle of utilities, the various product components which make up the bundle can be identified and isolated. It should be recognized that a product can thus be bundled or unbundled accordingly.

Bundling is a strategy which combines a number of benefits—made available usually at a lower total price than if each benefit were separately purchased. The rule in most cases is for a company to gain the upper hand on its competitors by offering a larger and better bundle of benefits. The credit card business serves as a good example. American Express, Visa, and MasterCard all try to outdo each other by offering a benefit bundle which includes guaranteed hotel reservations, credit card registration, cash advances, lost card replacement, free travel accident insurance, ATM access, personalized access checks, and twenty-four-hour customer service. American Express has gone so far as to offer its cardholders an extended warranty on products which they bought by charging the purchases to their American Express cards. As would be expected, the benefit bundle of a premium credit card (gold card) is better than that of a regular card.

Although bundling is usually a preferred strategy, some positive points can be made for unbundling. In several instances, it makes good marketing sense to unbundle a product so that a customer is not saddled with a high price and other unneeded benefits. Unbundling allows the customer to purchase only the desired benefit without being forced to pay for other combined benefits which are irrelevant. If the securities brokerage business is considered as an example, it was a widespread practice to charge customers a fixed price for a total service bundle which included investment advice regardless of whether the customer wanted it or not. Since deregulation, however, investors now have a choice. They can maintain the same extent of service as in the past by using such full-service brokers as Merrill Lynch and Dean Witter. On the other hand, discount brokers such as Quick & Reilly and Charles Schwab have thrived by offering to only execute orders for a much smaller fee. The reduced bundle, without advice and other frills, is exactly what many investors want.

Companies may pursue different bundling strategies. The bundling variations are usually dictated by the existence of multiple market segments. As illustrated by service stations, full-service gas stations' prices are relatively high because these service stations cater to that market segment which is not very price sensitive and which demands more services. Many consumers, however, do not require such services—at least not on a routine basis. Self-service stations have thus unbundled their service offering so that these stations can use their lower prices to appeal to price-sensitive motorists. Their low prices are made possible by the elimination of such extras as pumping gas, water hose inspection, washing windows, tire and oil checks, and so forth. If customers want to use credit cards, self-service stations generally charge extra for this added benefit.

Compaq has successfully competed with IBM by offering a larger bundle of utilities for the same price. Compaq's aim is to give customers, among other things, more memory and speed for their money. IBM, in contrast, has traditionally employed the unbundling approach, which allowed its dealers to make profit on accessories. The new IBM PS/2 machines, however, have upset some dealers because these machines have many more functions and accessories already built in, giving dealers less opportunity to sell such items as disk drives or monitors to generate profit.

The effectiveness of the bundling approach may be dictated in part by a product's life cycle. In 1984, Apple Computer bundled two applications programs into its Macintosh package because of software unavailability. Buyers could thus get Macwrite and Macpaint (for word processing and drawing) at no additional charge. But when the machine gained wider acceptance and thousands of programs became available, Apple's Macintosh package was subsequently unbundled, and Macwrite and Macpaint were thereafter sold for $125 each.

It is an unsound practice to haphazardly assemble a bundle. Some product features may be useless or meaningless, and their addition adds nothing but cost and confusion to the bundle. The bundle thus must be examined from time to time to determine its suitability. The approach used by Borg-Warner merits consideration. The company uses "value analysis," which focuses less on a product's tangible aspects and more on the product's function as desired by its customers.[2] Ford, as a customer, was asked to identify product features and functions important for its valve recirculating exhaust gas. Once known, Borg-Warner set up a team consisting of representatives from such diverse areas as marketing, management, purchasing, engineering, and the production line. The team's mission was to identify the function and cost of every part of the valve mechanism. Those of little value to Ford were then changed or deleted from the bundle.

PRODUCT VS. COMMODITY

It is important to make the distinction between a product and a commodity. A *commodity* is an undifferentiated product, whereas a *product* is a value-added and differentiated commodity.[3] This distinction is critical because the promotion and pricing strategies for the two concepts vary greatly.

Agricultural commodities, for example, usually do not require brand promotion because farmers may not be able to differentiate their product offerings. Any promotion would thus serve only to add unnecessary costs. The lack of product differentiation, then, does not provide sellers with an opportunity to deviate from market prices. Pricing flexibility (e.g., premium pricing) is therefore more likely to be found in the case of a product.

Although agricultural items are inherently commodities, several farm co-ops have learned to use such marketing techniques as advertising and product differentiation to turn their commodities into products. The $32 billion branded co-ops have successfully utilized marketing to add value to their agricultural commodities. Blue Diamond Growers, for instance, has spent $8 million a year on promotion of its flavored almonds. By building brand name recognition, most major co-ops can pay their member farmers more than the market price for their crops.

Commodities are not only restricted to agricultural items. Most personal computers are remarkably similar, and their high-tech nature does not make them less of a commodity. This is one reason why IBM abandoned the PC market and moved on to the proprietary PS/2 system. Airlines' services, likewise, are essentially commodities, making price competition inevitable.

It is worthwhile, whenever possible, to transform a commodity into a product. As explained by Ian Wilson, Castle & Cooke's president and chief executive officer, "When you're dealing with commodities, you can get shot at the knees." Water can serve as an illustration. Tap water is a commodity, costing only a fraction of a penny per gallon. But when water is converted into a product, it can command a price which is several hundred times higher.

How can water be made into a product? A water marketer can do so by adding value to its basic water commodity in many different ways. First, by bottling it, bottled water can be conveniently bought, carried, and transported. Second, bottled water can be promoted as a necessity by playing on the fear of deteriorating tap water. Next, water can be promoted and sold as a luxury with a snob appeal. Perrier has done a remarkable job in promoting its sparkling mineral water as a status beverage. Canada Dry, attempting to do the same, has repositioned its bottled water—from a mixer to a stand-alone drink. Finally, some water marketers try to add value in the form of flavor (e.g., lemon-lime "flavored" water).

PRODUCT LEVELS

In modern marketing, a marketer takes too narrow a perspective if the competition is only viewed at the product brand level. More often than not, the marketer faces multi-level product competition rather than single-level product competition. As such, the marketer finds that it is necessary to compete at each and every product level. As a result, it is necessary and desirable for the marketer to be familiar with and to distinguish between the five product levels: product mix, product line, product form, product class, and product brand.

A company's *product mix* or product portfolio consists of all products marketed by the firm regardless of whether they are related or not. *Reader's Digest*'s product mix, for example, includes magazines, hardcover books, records, music tapes, audio equipment, educational materials, fund-raising operations, and such assorted items as globes and maps that can be sold by mail. Hearst's product mix, as another example, goes beyond the well-known newspaper division, since it includes software for cable TV, videodiscs, and cassettes, not to mention such popular magazines as *Cosmopolitan*, *Good Housekeeping*, and *House Beautiful*.

General Mills's product mix, in contrast, at one time or another, consisted of such diverse products and services as Betty Crocker cake mixes, Big G cereals, Gold Medal flour, Gorton's seafoods, approximately 440 Red Lobster restaurants and 165 other restaurants under other names, Yoplait yogurt, Eddie Bauer, the more-than-130-store Talbots chain, Izod-LaCoste, Parker Brothers, and Kenner Products. As a result of the wide diversity of products offered, the company has recently been reorganized along three product lines: consumer foods, restaurants, and specialty retailing. In 1988, General Mills, in its attempt to divest itself of the Specialty Retailing Group, sold Talbots to Jusco Co. of Japan for $325 million and Eddie Bauer to Spiegel for $260 million. General Mills's strategy was to concentrate on its other two businesses, packaged foods and restaurants, because its sales came primarily from these businesses.

A company's product mix may have several product lines. Whereas a product mix may have related as well as unrelated products, a *product line* is a group of *related* products. Each SBU (strategic business unit) can also be considered a product line. The case of Greyhound, for example, involves a $3-billion, multi-industry company offering four basic lines: consumer products, financial services, services, and transportation and manufacturing. American Express, likewise, has four basic lines: travel-related services (American Express Travel Related Services Company), investment banking (Shearson Lehman Brothers), private banking (American Express Bank Ltd.), and financial planning services (IDS Financial Services Inc.).

Products can be related in a number of different ways. They can be related because they are sold together (e.g., hamburger and a drink), they are used together (socks and shoes), or they are made together using the same materials, equipment, technology, or labor. If a line of audio products is taken as an example, the product line consists of such product classes as receivers, speakers, turntables, and tape decks, all of which perform complementary functions related to sound reproduction.

Within each product line, there are usually a group of product classes (or categories). A *product class* is a particular product designed to serve a specific purpose or function. A stereo receiver is a product class which performs the functions of receiving and amplifying an audio signal. The speaker, another product class, has the task of reproducing the sound. A turntable, on the other hand, has the function of rotating and playing a record. A tape recorder, in comparison, can both record and play back the sound.

A product class often assumes a number of *product forms*. Such forms may differ in terms of shape, dimension, and other engineered characteristics. Yet all of these variations, regardless of their physical characteristics or appearance, still perform the same function. Tape decks, for example, come in a variety of shapes and sizes. Some are portable; some are not. Some are large, while others are small. Some are for automobile use; some are for home use. Some are for amateurs; others are for professionals and studio use. In addition, the three basic tape recorder forms are 8-track, cassette, and reel-to-reel (open reel). Although they are physically different, they all perform the same basic function: recording and playing back sound. Each medium can even assume a distinct image. The cassette form is perceived to be superior in sound quality to the 8-track but inferior to the open reel. Yet all three are threatened by a new technological form: DAT (digital audio tape), not unlike conventional turntables being replaced by the more advanced CD players.

Product forms can also be direct competitors in the sense that they serve as alternatives in satisfying the same need. Because product forms are close substitutes, a buyer of one product form is unlikely to be interested in a competing product form. Thus, the market gain of one product form usually comes at the expense of another. For example, there has been a steady loss of market share for whisky blends, bourbons, and Scotch in favor of vodkas and rums. Seagram has been slow to recognize this fact and has fallen behind in the two fast-growing vodka and rum product forms. One reason for this development has been Sam Bronfman of Seagram disliking vodka, feeling that it is too simple a product.

Within the deodorant product industry, according to the January 6, 1987, issue of *Drug Topics*, the popular forms of deodorant and their dollar market share of the $934-million-per-year industry were as follows: stick (33 percent), roll-on (31 percent), aerosol (32 percent), and all others (4 percent). The breakdown of analgesics by product form based on market share is: tablets (68.3 percent), caplets (24.3 percent), liquids (2.6 percent), drops (2.1 percent), powders (2.1 percent), capsules (0.5), and granules (0.1 percent). It is important to note the drastic decline of the popularity of the capsule product form after the poisoning episodes involving Tylenol. Furthermore, the fall of capsules was accompanied by the rise of caplets.

Because of consumers' varying buying motives, even for the same need, a company may find it necessary to offer more than one product form to satisfy customers' varying preferences. Kraft, for example, competes with other companies on five of the seven margarine type products. The company's margarine and margarine-substitute products are stick margarine, tub margarine, squeeze margarine, margarine substitute spread, and diet margarine. These various product forms of margarine not only compete with each other but also with the butter product class.

Within each product form, there are usually a large number of competing brands. A *product brand* is a particular product form offered by a certain firm. Some of these brands pit one company against another, whereas other brands are owned by the same company and compete among themselves. Procter & Gamble, for example, has a number of brands of detergent, and these brands include Gain, Tide, Bold, Oxydol, Cheer, Duz, Dreft, and Dash. The company has done a good job of endowing each brand with a unique personality (image) even though these brands are not chemically different. Tide is the all-purpose detergent which overpowers dirt by brute force. Cheer is for all-temperature washing. Oxydol, on the other hand, has oxygen bleach. In the case of Dreft, it is a light-duty detergent that is soft for the hands.

The candy industry provides a good example of brand competition within and across companies. M & Ms/Mars's brands of candies include M & Ms, Mars, Snickers, and Milky Way, which compete not only with each other but also against Hershey's brands and R. J. Reynolds's Baby Ruth and Butterfinger product brands. In the case of Maytag, the company also owns such brands as Magic Chef, Hardwick Stove, Jenn-Air, Admiral, and Norge. Interestingly, the company planned to offer refrigerators under all of these brands for every market segment.

Marketers should understand these different product levels, because they may have to compete with other companies on each and every product level. Consumers after all have limited incomes, and firms must compete for consumers' scarce resources. Although PepsiCo and Coca-Cola have created a great deal of publicity through their "cola wars," they have also waged a battle on other fronts by way of their product mixes, which include snacks, foods, and other beverages. The two tobacco giants, R. J. Reynolds and Philip Morris, have also battled each other beyond the cigarette product class, since their product mixes include other product classes such as soft drinks and alcoholic beverages. Their cigarette competition includes such product forms as full flavor, menthol, low tar, and varied lengths (85s, 100s, and 120s). At the brand

Exhibit 1.2
R. J. Reynolds Industries' Product Mix—Selected Products

Product mix: more than 200 brands in 39 product categories

Product line: tobacco (R. J. Reynolds Tobacco Co.), food (Nabisco Brands, Inc., Del Monte Corporation, and Kentucky Fried Chicken Corp.), and beverages (Nabisco Brands, Inc., and Heublein Inc.)

Product class: cigarette, cigar, smoking tobacco, cookies, crackers, candy bar, bubble gum, peanuts, ice cream, fruit, vegetable, soft drink, cocktail, club soda, seltzers, tonic, steak sauce, margarine, oriental foods, Mexican foods, frozen foods, baking powder, cereals, yeast, corn oil, mustard, pie fillings, dog biscuits, desserts, spirits, and wine

Product form: cigarette—hard pack, soft pack, 85s, 100s, 120s, menthol, filtered; cookies and snacks—fruit chewy cookies, chocolate chip cookies, shortbread, wafers, sandwich cookies, pretzels; spirits—cognac, Scotch whisky, Canadian whisky, liqueur, tequila, gin, vodka, wine, wine cooler, imported wine, and beer

Product brand: Winston, Vantage, Salem, Camel, More, NOW, Almost Home, Chips Ahoy, Nabisco, Ritz, Mister Salty, Sunkist, Canada Dry, Hawaiian Punch, Cheese Nips, Premium, Baby Ruth, Beech-Nut, Bubble Yum, Planters, Del Monte, A.1., Blue Bonnet, Chun King, Fleischmann's, and Life Savers

---

level, Philip Morris's brands include Marlboro, Virginia Slims, and Merit. R. J. Reynolds, in contrast, offers such brands as Winston, Vantage, Camel, Salem, and More. Exhibit 1.2 lists some of R. J. Reynolds Industries' products at each level.[4]

MANAGEMENT OF PRODUCT MIX

The management activities dealing with a company's product mix should begin with an examination of its breadth and depth. The breadth of a product mix is measured by the company's product lines—the greater the number of product lines, the broader the mix. The depth, on the other hand, is indicated by the variations (number of product classes/forms/brands within each line)—the greater the variations, the deeper the mix. In planning the company's product mix, it is prudent not to make the mix too broad or too narrow. Furthermore, this mix should be neither too deep nor too shallow.

The Breadth of a Product Mix

Product mix should not be too narrow in order to avoid putting all the "eggs in one basket." The consequence of this kind of planning may be that any unfavorable shift in demand can create an adverse impact.

This is also the problem faced by a firm whose business is cyclical in nature. As an example, the milk industry is currently facing problems such as fewer children wanting to drink milk and older consumers being diet conscious and avoiding high-fat dairy products. Dean Foods has been able to overcome this dilemma by broadening its product mix. The company has diversified into other refrigerated foods such as party dips, cranberry beverages, and Chocorific nondairy chocolate drinks.

It is also true that a company's product mix should not be too broad. It is important to know one's business and avoid being a Jack-of-all-trades or a conglomerate dealing in a variety of unfamiliar products. During the 1960s and 1970s, it was a widespread practice to become a conglomerate and acquire unrelated businesses based solely on financial considerations such as return on investment. The assumption was that the professional manager could manage any business—even an unfamiliar one. Experience has shown since then that the management of too many unrelated or unfamiliar businesses is anything but easy. This style of management stretches the ability of the executive to the limit, requiring too much general management time and not enough attention to specific problems dealing with the product, markets, distribution, and other problems of a more particular nature.

Uniroyal's venture into such businesses as golf balls, footwear, and industrial protective clothing turned out to be a financial drain and a large disappointment. Because it was involved in a large number of diverse product areas, Uniroyal's management failed to react at the right time and missed an opportunity to capitalize on its strong Keds brand name in the footwear business.

There now seems to be pressure to deconglomerate and move away from portfolio-style management. Beatrice Corporation has divested itself of some 50 businesses and consolidated the other 350 units into 30 divisions and six groups. Gillette's acquisitions in the 1970s of digital watches, calculators, leather goods, and smoke detectors also showed a lack of synergy. Recently the company has focused itself back on basics—to do what it knows best (i.e., razors and blades).

The current trend within product mix among diversifed companies is to carry out mergers and acquisitions on a more rational basis—that is, a diversified organization based on a core business. It is now an acceptable practice to divest operating units that have indefensible market positions, poor profits, or unsatisfactory growth. Gulf and Western, for example, has changed from a conglomerate to a focused operating company. In the process, it has disposed of some 25 businesses, ranging from racetracks to metals, that accounted for 20 percent of its assets.

One reason for Procter & Gamble's success is the fact that, despite the company's numerous products, the company is not a conglomerate. Its product mix is the result of a single, long, continuous evolution. The company's thorough knowledge of soap led to the addition of detergents and cleaners. Shampoo (Prell and Head & Shoulders) and toothpaste (Crest and Gleem) soon followed. Along the same line, Procter & Gamble's oil technology led to Jif peanut butter. After learning the roasting and processing techniques, it acquired the Folger's coffee brand. In another case, the company's knowledge of wood pulp led to such products and brands as Charmin, White Cloud, Bounty, Puffs facial tissues, and Pampers diapers.

The Depth of a Product Mix

A company should not offer a product mix which is too shallow. The mix is too shallow when the company does not have adequate product varieties or selection (in terms of product classes, forms, or brands). Cooper Vision has been able to move ahead of competitors by giving physicians a wide variety of eye care products. The diversity of its line helps to lower costs by spreading overhead expenses. This strategy also helps to lower eye doctors' costs and saves them time, thus winning their loyalty.

When a market consists of multiple market segments, a shallow mix will exclude many potential buyers due to an inadequate availability of styles, prices, sizes, and so forth. Without convenience and selection, consumers have difficulty trading up, down, or sideways. It is thus difficult for a company to maintain the loyalty of dealers and consumers. American Motors's problems can be attributed in part to its limited mix (mainly of small cars), making it difficult for its dealers to compete with Detroit's big three (General Motors, Ford, and Chrysler) which all have deeper mixes (i.e., a complete lineup of virtually all car types).

The problem of depth is further compounded if demand happens to be shifting away from the limited mix. Munsingwear, for example, at one time was in serious difficulty for having only a few product lines. VisiCorp serves as another good example. This company once derived half of its revenues from Visicalc, a popular but aging product which was threatened by such superior spreadsheet programs as Lotus 1–2–3. This problem of a shallow product mix led to the company's losses of several million dollars.

A deep product mix, on the other hand, can sometimes offer a company a unique strategic position. Timkens, for instance, has a product line that is so deep that it is difficult for any U.S. or foreign companies to compete with it. No competitor can offer the same assortment as Timkens's 26,000 bearing combinations because the cost of tooling up for a single new bearing series can be as high as $200,000. Timkens, in addition, offers superior service and technological support.

In general, however, a company's product mix should not be too deep.

Too deep a mix is a sign of oversegmentation. Too many product variations can have the tendency of confusing the manufacturer, dealers, and consumers alike. The consequences of an oversegmentation of a market are unnecessary investment and duplication of resources.

Some may argue that each product variation or version is justified because there is a demand for it. The problem with this point of view is that cannibalization may result. It should be understood that if there are a large number of product varieties being produced, these varieties often compete to replace each other because they are interdependent. Although consumers may prefer one product version to another, consumers are usually willing to settle for a reasonable alternative that performs the most critical functions adequately even if the alternative does not fit consumers' needs exactly. Consumers do not need to select from a dozen colors of appliances, for example. Sunbeam actually won applause from its retailers when it reduced the number of colors of its small appliances from nine to one, simplifying its dealers' inventories and consumers' decisions.

When market segments are independent, each segment must be examined based on its own worth. Steel, according to some, is a dying industry. U.S. Steel, realizing this, had to make several adjustments. Although still wanting to remain the largest U.S. steel producer in the year 2000, U.S. Steel made the decision not to participate in every single market. Subsequently, it pruned such product lines as ax bar and rod operations and tin mill products. The corporate name was also changed to USX to reflect the company's new direction.

Product Mix Surveillance

A company's product mix should be kept under constant surveillance. An effective product mix used in the past may not be effective for present or future markets. IBM's product mix, for example, has changed to keep pace with high-growth segments. During the 1960s and 1970s, IBM's mainframe computers accounted for 60–70 percent of the company's business. In the 1980s, that percentage has since been cut by more than half. This was a reasonable decision for IBM because of the fast growth of small computers, terminals, and communication equipment. Likewise, American Bakeries, recognizing the trend toward diet consciousness, has shifted its product mix from consisting of 60 percent white bread and rolls to other baked products made from natural and whole grains.

Due to the highly competitive nature of the U.S. tire market, several tire makers have reduced their reliance on the tire business. Uniroyal, for example, has planned to alter its product mix from the 48–26–26 percent split among the three divisions consisting of tires, engineered products and services, and chemicals. The new split envisioned is a 40–20–40 percent, with the first two divisions shrinking in importance. The tire division has eliminated radial truck tires and non-Uniroyal-brand tires, while the production of passenger and light truck tire lines was halved, reducing the company's inventory by 40 percent.

CONCLUSION

Product is in reality a broad concept which is often defined too narrowly. In addition to a product's physical configuration and explicit performance, its implicit attributes and performance must be carefully considered. Most tangible products have both explicit and implicit characteristics. The explicit characteristics are physical in nature (e.g., shape, weight, size, etc.), and their functions are more or less obvious. However, the product also has implicit characteristics that provide a particular reward or benefit related to consumer expectation, and this reward is associated with one brand but not necessarily with another. Therefore, the product will include symbolic meaning such as convenience, price, service, brand name, and other attributes not often obviously recognized.

Opportunities can be needlessly lost due to the failure to properly define a product. The wise marketer must define the product in terms of the present and potential benefits desired by customers—the more benefits, the better. The effective marketing of any product or service must thus begin with a precise definition of the product.

A product should also be envisioned as a bundle of satisfactions. The bundle can be adjusted in terms of promotion, place (distribution), and price to fit the various market segments. A better bundle has strategic advantage since it provides consumers with more reasons to purchase the product. However, additional attributes and benefits do cost money, and those attributes with minimal contribution in product value may be unnecessary and should be deleted from the bundle. In any case, for the different bundling and unbundling approaches to coexist, the market must consist of diverse, viable segments.

When compared to a product, a commodity generally consists of a smaller benefit bundle. As a result, the commodity seller usually has to conform to market forces and prices beyond his control. Better pricing control and flexibility can be achieved only when a commodity is transformed into a meaningful product.

Companies do not compete solely at the brand level. A proper perspective of competition involves an appreciation of multi-level marketing decisions related to product mix, product line, product class, product form, and product brand. These different product levels, being highly related, compete with each other for consumers' preferences and re-

sources. Small companies may choose to specialize on some but not all
product levels. Large companies, in contrast, must consider the effect
of a decision at one level on product performance at another level. A
certain product level may be set up as an independent SBU to compete
on its own, while other levels may be designed to be more integrated.
Also, due to the interdependence of nations, companies may eventually
be forced to compete in more than one market or country. Their actual
product lineups may differ from country to country due to the competitive strengths and weaknesses in each market. Ultimately, companies
will have to learn how to compete based on their total global resources
and product mixes.

NOTES

1. Theodore Levitt, *The Marketing Imagination* (New York: Free Press, 1983).

2. "The Revival of Productivity," *Business Week*, 13 February 1984, pp. 92ff.

3. For discussion of branding implications and strategies, see Sak Onkvisit
and John J. Shaw, "The International Dimension of Branding: Strategic Considerations and Decisions," *International Marketing Review*, forthcoming.

4. R. J. Reynolds Industries 1985 Annual Report.

2

Product Development

NECESSITY OF AND REASONS FOR NEW PRODUCTS

Given the high risk associated with the introduction of new products, it may seem surprising at first that companies continue to introduce new products. In 1986, 2,530 new food products were introduced. Some 10,000 new products were marketed in 1987. Between 1980 and 1985, Campbell alone added more than 300 new products. In the case of Nabisco Brands, more than 100 new products and line extensions were added in 1985. The effort, in most cases, is a logical one due to a number of reasons.

First, a matter of survival and growth is involved. Experience has shown that many of the products within a company's product mix will decline in popularity over time. When Atari initially went into business, Atari's first and only product was Pong. When the demand for Pong began to fade, Atari very wisely added other electronic products.

Since few companies can survive by remaining static, they must seek growth—often through new products. According to a *Better Homes and Gardens* survey, 53 percent of consumers bought a new product in the past month, and 43 percent did so in the past ten days. Compared with other fast-food competitors, McDonald's has done a superb job of maintaining its growth through additions of such new products as breakfast items and Chicken McNuggets and the addition of new outlets.

Growth, it should be realized, can be absolute as well as relative. It is possible for a company to grow absolutely in terms of sales volume while losing ground relatively in terms of market share. Apple Computer, although growing impressively almost continuously each year in terms of sales and revenues, lost ground to IBM when IBM entered the personal computer market. To regain market share, Apple tried to out-innovate IBM by introducing new products such as the Macintosh line of computers. Ironically, after dominating the personal computer market, IBM began to lose market share to the lower-priced clones. As a result, IBM itself had to switch to its new PS/2 system.

Because the market is dynamic, changes in regulations and related industries should be anticipated and expected. These changes can make existing products obsolete and new ones necessary. Banks and savings and loan associations, once without other forms of competitors, were able to take advantage of the market by offering low-interest-rate checking and savings accounts to lure low-cost deposits. After deregulation, the situation changed drastically. Nonbank financial institutions gained market share by offering attractive money market funds accounts. Ultimately, banks and savings and loan associations were forced to introduce their own money market accounts to compete with nonbank financial institutions. Had banks and savings and loan associations not been so complacent (and greedy), there would likely not have been any need for a new breed of competitors to "invent" higher-cost money market funds.

A company may seek sales stability by creating new products to diversify its risks. The basic idea of this strategy is to avoid having all the "eggs in one basket." Some existing products may have sales which, by nature, are cyclical or seasonal. In such cases, a new product can fill in and smoothen the cycles or seasons. Sun-Diamond, attempting to reduce its sales cyclicality, has deliberately made walnuts less of a holiday product by promoting chopped walnuts as a year-round item for home baking. Since the demand for soft drinks is seasonal, Coca-Cola has moved into the movie and wine businesses (without much success, however), and Pepsi is in such businesses as snacks, sporting goods, and restaurants (Pizza Hut).

Maturing markets are another reason for adding new products. Through the diversification process new products are produced and these products generate a new kind of demand. Tobacco companies started diversifying long before the heated and determined efforts to ban smoking began in the 1980s. Philip Morris owns Miller beer, and R. J. Reynolds has acquired Nabisco and Del Monte. Because the ready-to-eat cereal market is mature, Kelloggs decided to diversify into a new market with Whitney's yogurt.

Ironically, as new products are marketed, these new products force companies to come up with even more new products. The massive proliferation of new consumer goods shortens the life cycle of existing products while increasing marketing costs. With more choices, consumers are readily inclined to become less brand loyal. Such brand indifference only forces manufacturers to create new products to keep their customers. It is thus not surprising that half of the almost 300 cigarette brands and varieties which currently exist in the market came from products that did not exist ten years ago. Gillette, likewise, recently disclosed that half of its 1982 revenues was derived from products which were less than five years old.

When a new product achieves a success in the market, it can make a very significant contribution to the company's earnings. Coleco's 1983 sales were $596 million. But with the addition of Cabbage Patch dolls to the company's product mix, the company's earnings soared. Subsequently, the figures showed that Cabbage Patch dolls single-handedly accounted for nearly 30 percent of the company's sales and profits. By 1986, however, Cabbage Patch products began to decline in popularity, forcing Coleco to search for a new winner, apparently without much success. By 1988, the problem was so severe that the company had to consider filing for bankruptcy protection. Coleco's spectacular success and decline could thus be attribted in part to the fact that the company was largely a one-product company.

PROBLEMS OF NEW PRODUCTS

Most, if not all, marketers will surely and readily agree that it is anything but easy to come up with a successful product. As commented

in 1988 by Nabisco Brands' executive vice president, less than 1 percent
of the 45,000 new products of the past 16 years had gained sales of $15
million annually. According to *The Wall Street Journal*, consumers encounter seven new products each day, but 94 percent of such food items
would soon leave the market.

Of thousands of new products introduced each year, the overwhelming majority will fail. For every winner, there are many losers. As commented by Arthur L. Fry, a scientist at 3M, "You've got to kiss a lot of
frogs to find a prince."

Among notable failures are such product forms as the midi and four-
channel sound system and such product brands as the Chevrolet Cor-
vair, Ford Edsel, and Real cigarette. Even very successful companies
such as Procter & Gamble and McDonald's are not exempt. McDonald's
failed with its Onion McNuggets and McRib, and Procter & Gamble was
disappointed by its Hidden Magic hairspray, Extend mouthwash, and
Teel toothpaste.

It is very common for a company to spend a great deal of time pre-
paring a product idea for market before the new product idea can find
its way to the market. Between new product proposal and nationwide
distribution, the time lapse can be several years. When an automaker
makes the commitment to a new car design, the actual production of
the car is four years away. Likewise, the development of a major new
drug can easily take ten years—in addition to the expenditure of $70
million.

The problem created by the lengthy gap between product design and
production ocurrs because of the dynamic nature of the market. During
the interval between product design and production, market factors may
change, the economy may turn unfavorable, and consumer tastes may
change. It is thus very advantageous to try to reduce the time period
between inception of a new product idea and product introduction.
Xerox, for example, was able to use a new product development process
to reduce the time it took to bring a new copier to the market from 65
months to 51 months.

It should be apparent that the considerable length of time for a product
to reach the market incurs a high degree of risk, not unlike the rolling
of dice and not knowing what to expect. Anticipation and prediction
should thus be a necessary part of the product development process.
As commented by one executive, "Developing a new product is like
shooting a duck. You can't shoot it where it is; you've got to shoot it
where it's going to be."

The high cost of introducing a new product is another reason why
new product ventures are a high-risk proposition. It is difficult in today's
market to introduce a national brand in a major product category for
less than $50 million. Procter & Gamble, for example, spent $100 million

introducing its Citrus Hill orange juice to market, and this was a relatively simple product.

The penalty for a market failure is also very great. Coleco, for example, was forced to write off $119 million for its ill-fated Adam home computer. Mattel did not fare any better, as its home computer lost $361 million. Polaroid lost $68 million on its Polavision instant movie system. Federal Express had to absorb $350 million in losses and write-offs because of the failure of its Zap-Mail. After spending 15 years in research and development for its videodisc players, RCA realized that there was no "real" demand for this product. After all was said and done, the company realized this $780 million too late.

The fate of USA Today and the Discover credit card have been uncertain. Since introducing USA Today in 1982, Gannett has had to put up with a string of yearly operating losses to the tune of $300–350 million. These losses do not even include the salaries of the editorial staff who are on loan from Gannett's other papers. Sears, likewise, understood that it had to invest $400 million in bringing its Discover credit card to market. Sears was thus not surprised when there were losses of more than $100 million for each of the first two years, mainly from development costs.

NEW PRODUCTS BASED ON RISK AND REWARD

New products can be classified according to the degree of risk, expense, and reward.[1] The first type is known as line extension or flankers. This new-product strategy has the lowest degree of risk because the brand name is familiar and has achieved efficiencies in production, distribution, and promotion. Kraft, although already producing Philadelphia Brand, the top-selling cream cheese, introduced spreadable Soft Philly, offered more flavors, added Philadelphia Lite, and used the brand for its pourable salad dressing. Pepperidge Farm, happy with the performance of its American Collection Cookies in the premium baked goods category, quickly added frozen microwavable American Collection Desserts as a line extension.

A potential problem with the line extension strategy is the risk of cannibalization which may occur to the parent brand. As such, line extensions are suitable only when they offer higher margins than existing products or when they are used to stave off competition.

The second strategy entails the creation of a new brand in a familiar category. Quaker Company, for example, has canned and burger-type dog and cat foods but did not have products available in the growing dry pet food product category. It thus introduced Tender Chunks as a premium brand in order to fill this gap in its product line.

The last new-product strategy includes the introduction of a new business altogether. Kraft, for example, introduced A La Carte Entrees in a pouch, which do not require freezing or a long preparation time. Its La Creme frozen whipped topping is another example of a new product line. In the case of Dial Corp., its Lunch Buckets was a pioneer in a new product category of shelf-stable, microwavable meals as a convenient alternative to frozen and canned foods. A new product of this kind involves more risk than the first two product categories, but the high risk is usually accompanied by a higher degree of potential reward.

In 1987, according to the American Marketing Association, the ten best new products based on marketplace success and innovativeness were: Certified Stainmaster carpet, Bull's Eye barbecue sauce, O.N.E. dry dog food, Optima card, Sundance Natural Juice Sparkler, Acura Legend, Lunch Buckets, American Collection Cookies, Cherry 7Up, and Fab 1 Shot.[2]

Fortune, on the other hand, has its own list of top new products of 1987 that satisfied consumer needs while rewarding the companies marketing these products. The thirteen new products on *Fortune*'s list were: Acura Legend, Stainmaster carpet, disposable cameras (by Fuji and Kodak), Lifestyle condoms, Interplak electric toothbrush, DAT (digital audio tape) machines, Sparc computer chip, Mevacor drug, SF-4000 pocket computer, people meters, Equity CDs (certificates of deposit), miniskirts, and Optima card.

PRODUCT DEVELOPMENT PROCESS

It is generally accepted that product development consists of six related and distinct steps: (1) idea generation, (2) idea screening, (3) business analysis, (4) pilot development, (5) test marketing, and (6) commercialization.

Idea Generation

New product ideas can come from a variety of sources. Other than ideas which can come from the marketing staff's brainstorming sessions, new concepts can also come from salesmen, other nonmarketing employees, consultants, middlemen, the industry, competitors, publications, and so forth. One of Black and Decker's new products includes a heavy-duty reciprocating power saw which has a blade that moves back and forth and is used for cutting through plaster walls. This idea came from Acme Tool and Specialty which is a member of Black and Decker's dealer advisory council.

3M developed a special automobile masking tape after its salesman noted the difficulty experienced by autoworkers in keeping paints from running together on two-tone paint combinations for cars. Its Scotchgard fabric protector was developed from a lucky accident. 3M's chemist, while mixing an experimental liquid, accidentally spilled some on her tennis shoes. Further investigation and experimentation revealed that the treated sneakers were able to repel water and dirt.

Consumer frustration should be seriously considered because consumer complaints mean that there is something wrong with existing products. One writer for *Metropolitan Home* and *House Beautiful* asked the following questions, which were based on his frustrating experiences with many household products.[3] "Wouldn't automatic dishwashers be easier to use if they were modeled after built-in wall ovens and you didn't have to stoop to unload or load them? Why are door knobs so plentiful and popular, and levers so rare when levers are much easier to use? Why are shower control knobs located directly under shower nozzles so that you get doused with cold water when you turn them on? Has anybody invented a no-fog bathroom mirror, and, if so, why isn't it in every home in America?" Questions such as these are important and offer new product ideas and marketing opportunities.

Idea Screening

The sources of ideas are less important than the acknowledgement, review, and screening of such ideas—in a timely and efficient fashion. Campbell Soup Co. has weekly meetings to review ideas from all sources. Those ideas deemed potential and feasible are further studied. Consumer reaction can also be used as a screening criterion. New advertisements based on the product concept under consideration can also be created and shown to potential users in order to determine reaction and interest. This technique is better than merely providing a description of the product idea.

Airwick makes use of consumer interviews to measure new product ideas. If potential is indicated, the company then prepares a product sample and a video commercial to study consumer response. Because of the consumer input, none of its products has been introduced without some change to the original product idea. Its Carpet Fresh, conceived as a granular product, became a powdery cleaner because market tests revealed that consumers did not want stray granules to lodge under furniture.

Business Analysis

This step requires an estimation of profit. Profit determination depends on a number of other factors which must also be estimated. These factors include demand, product features, performance requirements, and cost.

Airwick's new product criteria require a product to be a specialty as well as a noncommodity household product that will provide a margin for promotion while generating sales of $30–100 million annually and recouping investment costs in two years. These requirements have led the company to discard such commodities as plant care items, private-label fresheners, toilet bowl cleaners, and a fire extinguisher. Stick-Ups deodorizer, however, was able to meet all these criteria. The unique attribute of the product at the time it was accepted was that it was small enough to be hidden by adhering to surfaces.

Pilot Development

The purpose of this step is to determine production feasibility. Pilot models are created and produced in small quantities. This step is largely technical and is carried out by the engineering department. Since the pilot production is largely exploratory, alternative production methods and designs must be considered, and it is thus desirable to simply use general-purpose or existing equipment instead of investing heavily in expensive specialized equipment.

Xerox's development process begins with the ideas proposed by its strategic business unit.[4] These ideas are then quickly evaluated by small "product synthesis" teams. Those ideas which survive these teams are designed by several competing teams of designers. If the prototype model is unable to satisfy the defined goals, the idea is discarded. Xerox's 1045 copier, for example, could not meet cost goals, and it was rejected in spite of a $1 million investment. But if the product can enter the "go" mode, a product development team then takes the prototype through manufacturing.

Test Marketing

Before making a total production commitment to a new product, the product must be test marketed in a limited market or test city. The purpose of test marketing is to determine basic market interest, distribution acceptance, and a potential marketing mix. R. J. Reynolds's successful test marketing with its Vantage brand convinced the company that there was a demand for a low-tar cigarette category. In 1985, R. J. Reynolds did test marketing on its Ritz brand to evaluate the product concept of combining stylish imagery with a premium quality cigarette. Ritz, as the first U.S. cigarette associated with a world-famous fashion designer, used packaging and advertising which reflected the influence of Yves Saint Laurent. Female smokers' positive responses in the test market led to the national distribution of Ritz a year later.

On the other hand, for some unexplained reason, R. J. Reynolds did not test market its Real brand. Trumpeted as the most expensive cigarette brand at the time in terms of promotion expenditures, Real was a flop because test marketing was not carried out; this step would likely have revealed that the brand's "natural" appeal was weak.

Test marketing can also alert management of potential problems. Procter & Gamble's wet toilet tissue called Certain was poorly received in a test market. Consumers felt that Certain was too greasy. NIA Insurance, feeling that the concept was already well known, did not bother to do any testing for its Personal Umbrella program for the affluent. Most of those who responded to the direct mail campaign which was run asked for an umbrella, thinking that the company was an umbrella manufacturer.

What makes a test city a good test market? In general, a good test market is one which (1) has typical demographics, (2) has the necessary media, and (3) is self-contained or isolated in terms of population and media.

If the population of the city is not self-contained, the sales results may be too optimistic due to the fact that the city may gain population (e.g., shoppers, workers) from nearby cities in the daytime. If the city is not isolated in terms of media, the media coverage may extend over too wide an area in order to reach consumers outside the desired city test market area, resulting in promotion waste (i.e., high costs). Furthermore, customers in the test market may be influenced by outside information which may also contaminate the results. Based on these criteria, Sacramento is considered a good test market whereas Los Angeles and San Francisco are not.

Although test marketing can be a valuable marketing tool, it is not always essential nor desirable. Products which are poor candidates for test marketing are fad products, emulation products, and products racing against time.[5] Fad products are not worth the cost of test marketing, whereas it is difficult to track the sales of an emulation product which consumers purchase after seeing it being used by others. For products racing against time, test marketing is not feasible because competitors may gain access to the idea and immediately introduce the product to the market.

For low-risk products or line extensions, it is possible to dispense with test marketing. As an example, Salem, Vantage, and Merit cigarettes have Salem Lights, Vantage Ultra Lights, and Merit Ultras respectively as line extensions. Playtex, likewise, decided to forego the test marketing of its Jhirmack shampoo because it felt that the recognition of the brand was sufficiently strong to allow immediate national distribution. Its assumption has since indeed proven correct.

Another practical reason for bypassing test marketing relates to competitors. To safeguard trade secrets, Philip Morris prefers using a taste test panel to test marketing. The taste test panel method involves the testing of consumer reaction to new brands of cigarettes through many small groups. On the other hand, Philip Morris tries to learn information from the test marketing efforts of its competitors. For example, when R. J. Reynolds's test marketing of Vantage indicated that there was demand for a low-tar cigarette, Philip Morris rushed its Merit brand into the market without test marketing.

In the case of Colgate-Palmolive, it stung Procter & Gamble and Clorox, which were testing the market for throw-in detergent pouches, by rushing its Fab 1 Shot into the national market without test marketing. The product is a packet which contains laundry detergent, fabric softener, and an antistatic element. Colgate thus became the first company to nationally exploit the technical breakthrough by opening up a new market segment.

For established competitors, there is often low interest in a company's test marketing results and more interest in destroying the results of the test market study. Competitors may want to discourage and frustrate a potential newcomer by flooding the test market with their own samples, coupons, and advertising. As may be expected, using such tactics on a national scale is futile because of the prohibitive costs.

Commercialization

The last step in the new product development process is commercialization. This step involves the full-scale production and marketing of the product on a nationwide basis, assuming that the results of test marketing are favorable. Minnetonka carried out tests for its pump concept for Softsoap liquid soap across 12 cities. It found that the product gained retailers' acceptance easily because it was the first product form of its kind, offering retailers higher gross margins without product duplication. Once the product had gained a 5 percent market share goal in its test markets, Minnetonka felt sufficiently confident to seek national distribution.

The practice at the present time is to focus the expenditure of funds in the earlier stages of the product development process in order to detect unsuccessful products at an early point. Once a product reaches the commercialization stage after a thoroughly rigorous screening, it stands a better chance of being successful.

Procter & Gamble's creation and marketing of the disposable diaper provides a good illustration of the process of product development. The company initially acquired the idea of the disposable diaper from one of its engineers who, as a grandfather, found cloth diapers to be messy and smelly. To test the viability of this product concept, Procter & Gamble applied three basic criteria: a real need, potential demand, and scientific and technological ability.

Was there a real need for disposable diapers? To answer this question, Procter & Gamble used consumer research and asked thousands of mothers. The results obtained from home and telephone interviews, questionnaires, and group discussion panels indicated that the cloth diaper was uncomfortable for babies, not adequately dry, and messy. The need for an alternative was fully obvious. Furthermore, the potential demand appeared sizable as evidenced by some 15 billion diaper changes a year. Finally, the company had the expertise to address this need because of its familiarity with such absorbent paper products as towels, facial tissue, and toilet tissue. All three criteria were thus covered and met for the disposable diaper product concept.

Next, Procter & Gamble assigned a team of chemists and engineers to develop a product. The result was an absorbent and flushable diaper to be inserted in plastic pants. Dallas consumers, however, were hardly enthusiastic because the test product generated too much heat for their babies. The acceptance of the product concept came only after the plastic pant was replaced by a thin sheet of plastic which allowed for air circulation.

The pilot test used handmade disposable diaper products to gauge demand before Procter & Gamble would commit capital investment to heavy machinery for mass production. To see if the demand for the product was as great as estimated (i.e., 400 million diapers annually), Peoria (Illinois) was chosen for test marketing. The sales results in the test market were disappointing because the actual sales were only half of the projected figure.

At a crossroad, Procter & Gamble faced a decision of whether to abandon the project and waste the millions of dollars it had invested. After consideration, the company decided to test market again in Sacramento (California) with a new price of six cents apiece (instead of ten cents) to see if price resistance could be overcome. Better luck prevailed this time. The demand was so great that it took the company nearly 20 years to construct sufficient new plants to meet demand for national distribution. The product involved in all of this? Pampers, of course.

NEW-PRODUCT CRITERIA

To adequately and properly evaluate product concepts, a company should have a systematic procedure. Toward this end, criteria should be set for product evaluation. Such criteria are necessary because limited resources must be allocated among the various product options.

No single set of product criteria can be suitable for all companies or products. Also, it is difficult to list all relevant criteria. However, there are several product criteria which are both significant and relatively universal. These are the criteria against which almost all products can be judged.

Market Demand

The demand criterion is an obvious requirement. The extent of market demand must be large enough to make a reasonable profit possible. Airwick made the decision to go ahead with its Carpet Fresh (a rug cleaner and room deodorizer) because it was impressed with the market demographics. The company discovered that the number of households which had children and/or dogs and cats was very high. Almost 40 percent of all U.S. households have children. In the case of pets, 33 million homes have at least one dog, and 21 million homes at least one cat. Kelloggs, likewise, defined the yogurt market as being the same as the ice cream market. With 88 percent of the population eating ice cream, the company felt that the potential demand for its Whitney's yogurt was quite substantial.

For any product to be successful, it must satisfy a *real* need. Baskin-Robbins developed a ketchup-flavored ice cream, but it decided not to market it. This was likely a good decision since it was doubtful whether there was any real demand for a product which sounded so unappetizing. Equally doubtful was the demand for chocolate hair-styling gel and parsnip chips. Minnetonka, in contrast, understood consumers' frustration with messy, slippery, and unusable bars of soap. Seeing a real need, the company created Softsoap as a "soap without the soapy mess" to solve the problem.

Production Consistency

A company can greatly reduce the risk of new product variation if the new product can be fit into the company's existing production structure. The fit can be achieved in a number of ways, ranging from the sharing of equipment, facilities, labor, and raw materials to the use of by-products as input for the new product.

Production consistency allows the company to avoid costly investment related to the production of a new product whose demand is uncertain. Furthermore, production consistency will improve the company's economies of scale, thus lowering overall fixed costs per unit. Hearst Corporation, for example, introduced new products by using existing resources (information) to produce software for videodiscs, cassettes, and cable TV (e.g., programs about cooking, fashion, and decoration).

Sugar producers provide an illustration of how to lower costs by using such by-products as molasses and the fibrous by-product of the sugar cane stalk (bagasse).[6] U.S. Sugar, for example, made silage for cattle feed from bagasse. Sun-Diamond Growers of California, a 6,000–member cooperative, has also done remarkably well by creating new products which have production consistency. It added pure fruit juice blends to its product line to compete with artificially flavored Hi-C and Hawaiian Punch. What used to be waste has been turned into attractive products. Split or bruised fruit, once given or thrown away, has been transformed into snack and industrial products. Fruit bits can be added to breakfast products, while prune paste is used for Danish pastries. Raisin juice concentrate, on the other hand, is offered as a mold inhibitor and as a sweetener in industrial baking. As for substandard raisins, stems, and prune pits, these by-products are distilled into alcohol, fuel, or cattle feed.

Production consistency, although important, should not be overemphasized. Scott, for example, at one time was preoccupied with finding paper products that its machinery could make. As a result, it lost sight of what customers really needed.

Marketing Consistency

Whenever possible, a new product should go beyond the production fit to include the existing marketing structure. Marketing consistency is important because of the benefits derived from efficient distribution and promotion. The promotional and distribution costs can be greatly reduced due to gains in economies of scale in advertising, personal selling, storage, transportation, and customer service.

Playtex, by using its existing distribution network to market its Jhirmack shampoo, was able to eliminate heavy startup costs. Tambrands, with 220,000 retail outlets in place to carry its Tampax tampons and Maxithins pads, found it relatively easy to utilize this distribution system for its new over-the-counter products which allowed home testing for ovulation and pregnancy.

Warnaco, on the other brand, did not maximize the use of its Hathaway and Puritan distribution channels. When adding Hathaway Outerwear (men's sport jackets) and Hathaway Patch (women's casual apparel), the company set up new divisions. The divisions for these new products were costly and very likely unnecessary.

Ideally, a new product should offer both production consistency and marketing consistency. When both cannot coexist, a company should choose the consistency with *higher* costs. That is, if the cost of marketing a new product is greater than the cost of producing it, marketing consistency must take precedence over production consistency.

The importance of marketing consistency in relation to production consistency can be illustrated by U.S. automakers. Most automobile manufacturers at one time also produced a line of heavy appliances, reasoning that the production principles for appliances and those for automobiles were largely the same. Although the production assumption was basically correct, the similarity however did not extend to the appropriate marketing methods for these two products. Whereas appliances are low-margin and slow-moving products, automobiles are the opposite. It appears obvious to us today that it would be difficult to use a car salesman to sell refrigerators in an automobile showroom, but this is how appliances were once sold. Not surprisingly, one automaker after another withdrew from the appliance business after it became apparent that the marketing methods required were quite different for the two products. The main beneficiary of these adjustments was White Consolidated, which acquired Hupp (Gibson) from Studebaker, Philco from Ford, Kelvinator from American Motors, and Frigidaire from General Motors.

It should be pointed out that a new product which has marketing consistency can offer a great deal of marketing impact in more ways than one. By having a more complete product mix or line, a manufacturer should find more positive reception from retailers or distributors. One reason why Hiram Walker acquired Bacardi was to make its own liquor salesmen welcome by distributors who were interested in carrying Bacardi rum.

With the addition of new products which make the product line complete, the sales forces of both a manufacturer and his distributors should be more enthusiastic. Having more new products provides the salesmen with more income opportunity, and higher morale should follow. Finally, consumer loyalty is retained as well because consumers have more product varieties for selection.

Legal Considerations

In a litigation-prone U.S. society, a new product cannot be introduced without considering its legal implications in terms of consumer safety, monopoly, patent protection, and patent infringement. Baskin-Robbins made a decision not to introduce its Goody Goody Gumdrop ice cream flavor to the market. This decision reflected a concern by the company that this tutti-frutti ice cream might crack customers' teeth due to the tiny gumdrops contained in the ice cream.

Alleging patent infringement, Gillette sued Scripto for marketing a pen similar to Gillette's Eraser Mate, while Airwick, protecting its Carpet Fresh, sued Love My Carpet. Dean Witter ended up paying Merrill Lynch $1 million for setting up a service account similar to Merrill Lynch's patented Cash Management Account.

Kodak is another company that has had more than its share of litigation. Accusing Kodak of using new products to create a monopoly in the photography market, Berkey Co. (which used to be in the film-developing business) sued Kodak for not giving advance notice of Kodak's plan to market the Pocket camera and 110 film. More recently, Kodak was ordered to stop marketing its instant photography cameras and film and to pay Polaroid a huge sum of money for patent infringement.

The tobacco industry provides an illustration of a new-product dilemma faced by tobacco companies. R. J. Reynolds Tobacco Company invented a new cigarette design. This low-smoke, zero-tar cigarette has a tip which, although lit like a regular cigarette, is a porous, slow-burning sliver of carbon. During inhalation, heated air is drawn through a flavor capsule to pick up the taste of tobacco and a dose of nicotine without burning the tobacco. R. J. Reynolds Tobacco, however, had at least two problems. The first one was the Federal Drug Administration's power to regulate nicotine as a drug but not when nicotine is in tobacco products. Advanced Tobacco Products, for example, was ordered to withdraw its Favor brand, which has a plastic tube to administer nicotine as users inhale. Because there was no tobacco in Favor, the Federal Drug Administration considered it to be an unapproved drug. R. J. Reynolds Tobacco thus must make sure that the nicotine comes from the tobacco rather than the flavor capsule. Another problem with that safer cigarette is the issue of product liability. The new product will make it easier for smokers to sue the company for continuing to market other cigarettes known to be harmful.

Minimum Cannibalization

Because many new products are simply old products in new product form, it is almost certain that a new product may in some way undermine a company's existing products by cannibalizing the original products' market share. Whether Coors's addition of Coors Light was a good move depends on whether cannibalization was considered when the brand was introduced. By almost all accounts, Coors Light was a large success—except for the fact that most of the purchasers of Coors Light came from the customers of the original Coors.

Efforts should be made to keep cannibalization at a minimum. When diet Coke was introduced, it quickly became the number one sugar-free soft drink. This success did not come at low cost since diet Coke took sales away from Coca-Cola's other products. About 25 percent of diet Coke's sales were siphoned from Tab (the former number one in this category or product form), 16 percent from regular Coke, and 7 percent from Sprite. Fortunately, the other 52 percent of diet Coke's sales came from new customers and the brands of other companies. To prevent the further erosion of Tab's market share, Coca-Cola decided to promote diet Coke and Tab differently, with Tab aimed at the female market segment.

In the case of Cherry 7Up, cannibalization was minimal, with only 10 percent of its customers coming from those drinking the regular 7Up. Cherry 7Up's success is due to its ability to attract new consumers, primarily from the teen market.

Although cannibalization should be a matter of concern, this concern should not become an obsession. IBM, being concerned that the PC jr would take market share away from the PC, deliberately designed the PC jr to be a distinctly different product. Instead of designing a better product, IBM preferred to include such built-in limitations as a toylike keyboard unsuitable for word processing. PC jr thus achieved its goal of not cannibalizing sales of the larger PC machines but ended up crippling its own sales.

Usually, a two-to-one rule should be used to judge the value of a new product where cannibalization is a factor. For every one percentage point of market share lost by an original product, the new product must generate at least two percentage points. In the case of Ivory Soap, after Procter & Gamble added Ivory Liquid soap, the market share of the regular Ivory soap dropped from 18.9 percent to 18.5 percent. However, Ivory Liquid more than compensated for this loss with a gain of 3 percent in market share.

Product Uniqueness

A company can gain strategic advantage by adding a product which has unique features. "Me-too" products, especially those which enter the market late, usually have difficulty in gaining market acceptance. To avoid having to offer a new product at a price lower than the prices of pioneering competitors, the product should be given some meaningful positioning. Procter & Gamble's Always pads are unique in the sense that their size is only 70 percent as large as that of Johnson & Johnson's Stayfree product, making retailers more receptive to carrying the product due to its better return on shelf space.

Brown & Williamson was late in bringing a cigarette to market in the low-tar category and determined it needed something unique. It noticed that the existing low-tar brands used a filter which gave a bland taste because the filter diverted the smoke away from the taste buds. Brown and Williamson thus created a fluted filter for its Barclay brand. This unique filter with its unusual tunnel design allows the smoke to linger over the tongue, achieving the objective of reducing tar while giving more taste sensation than competing brands. This uniqueness in design helped Barclay break all sales records for the introduction of a new cigarette.

Procter & Gamble's marketing of Liquid Tide provides another good illustration of how various product criteria can be taken into consideration when developing uniqueness in a product. The fast growth of the liquid detergent market showed that there was a real demand for this product form. Despite the obvious advantage of production consistency and marketing consistency, Procter & Gamble had concern over whether it should introduce Liquid Tide since its introduction could jeopardize the market position of powdered Tide, long the number one detergent in the market. But fears of cannibalization were minimal because Procter & Gamble had not done well in the liquid detergent market segment, which was dominated by Wisk, not to mention the fact that powder detergents had been losing market share to liquids. Furthermore, Liquid Tide, in spite of its late entry, was not a "me-too product"—it contains twice as many active ingredients as its competitors in addition to a new molecule. By all accounts, Procter & Gamble's decision to market Liquid Tide was a correct one. Not only did Liquid Tide do well, but it also did not adversely affect the market held by powdered Tide.

CONCLUSION

For companies to survive and/or grow, they must introduce new products. A marketer's problem is not so much one of creating a new product but rather introducing a successful one. The penalty of having no new product can be just as great as having one which fails.

To develop a new product, the marketer should carry a new product concept through the six basic steps: idea generation, idea screening, business analysis, pilot development, test marketing, and commercialization. The high cost of introducing a new product makes it critical to put more emphasis on the earlier stages so that winners can be distinguished from losers early.

To judge the worth of a potential product, product criteria need to be determined. The criteria determined can be useful in identifying those product ideas which are superior in terms of profit maximization and risk minimization. As a general rule, one should realize that any criteria, no matter how good, cannot offer an absolute guarantee of success. Despite this fact, criteria can serve as useful guidelines where new products are being considered. If a number of criteria are being examined, they can at the very least guard against the mistake of having too strong a preoccupation with financial considerations.

Whenever possible, a new product should complement rather than replace other products in the company's product mix. With complementary products, the overall company product situation can be improved instead of harmed. A microwave oven, for example, complements rather than replaces its conventional counterpart.

It must be kept in mind that the criteria used to evaluate new products must be meaningful. When Xerox, as a small company at the time, first thought of the electrophotography technology for automatic copiers, its consultants concluded that there was no demand for this new product. Xerox decided to gamble with the product anyway, and the technology has since revolutionized the way people work.

The Xerox example illustrates why the product criteria that are useful in evaluating existing products or specific products may not apply to an idea which is totally new and drastically radical. A major lesson from this incident is that, for companies dealing with new products, no single set of criteria can be relevant to all products, especially when brand-new product concepts are involved. Naturally, criteria are not a substitute for superior managerial judgment.

NOTES

1. "Internally Developed Products Fraught with Many Risks and Potential Rewards," *Marketing News*, 24 December 1982.

2. "AMA Names 10 Best New Products of 1987," *Marketing News*, 28 March 1988, pp. 1, 16.

3. Michael Walsh, "Life Gets Complicated by Design," *San Jose Mercury News*, 2 July 1988.

4. "How Xerox Speeds Up the Birth of New Products," *Business Week*, 19 March 1984, pp. 58–59.

5. "To Test Market or Not? It Depends," *Food & Beverage Marketing*, June 1985, p. 29.

6. "What Makes Sun-Diamond Grow," *Business Week*, 9 August 1982, p. 83.

PART II

CONSUMER CHARACTERISTICS AND BEHAVIOR

3

Demographics

THE NEW AMERICA

Heavy beer drinkers are primarily 18- to 34-year-old males who drink more than 50 percent of all beer sold. Blessed with a growth of 37 percent in this beer drinking age group in the 1970s, far faster than the total population, beer consumption grew an impressive 48 percent. But in the 1980s, as the post–World War II babies outgrew this age bracket, the growth of this segment flattened. To counter this predictable and inevitable trend, brewers must search for products which can appeal to people who traditionally have not drunk much beer. Older drinkers want beers that are less filling and that taste different from those sold to today's younger market.

Just like brewing companies, Disney faced hard times. Devoted to serving the children's and family market, Disney has been successful in part because of the growth of its prized segment, the 5- to 13-year-old age group, from 14.7 percent of the nation's population in 1950 to 18.2 percent in 1960. More than a decade later, the segment had shrunk to 15 percent. To make matters worse, the group over 25 years of age avoids any movie with a Disney label. With new social mores putting strains on the family unit, Disney must solve the demographic dilemma by appealing to the faster-growing adult audiences. It made a decision to set up Touchstone as a company to produce PG movies, and several hit movies (e.g., Splash, Ruthless People) soon followed.

To fulfill the founder's lifelong dream, Disney opened the Experimental Prototype Community of Tomorrow (EPCOT) adjacent to Disney World in 1984. As a permanent world's fair, EPCOT is a 258-acre site split into two areas called Future World and World Showcase, with displays of prototype technologies for making life easier. To encourage major corporations' participation in this extravagant project, Disney's sales pitch was that the target audience would have the following demographics: They are older, wealthier, and more cosmopolitan than regular ticket buyers at amusement parks.

The beer and Disney examples make it clear that the nation's population composition changes over time, creating problems for some industries and opening new markets for others. To safeguard itself against unnecessary surprises, the company must analyze its customers' demographic characteristics and prepare to make adjustments to conform to the trends.

NEED FOR DEMOGRAPHICS

Long before giving attention to psychological factors, marketers have used demographics with some success to understand and predict market behavior. Abbreviated from demographic characteristics, demographics is a study of human populations with reference to vital statistics such as size, density, and location.

Why should researchers and marketers be interested in demographics? The study of demographics is necessary because consumer as well as industrial demand depends upon population factors. For every industry and product, virtually all its customers in the next decade and beyond presently exist. By looking closely at these people, a marketer can determine the kind of market it will have in the next two decades. Furthermore, psychological variables, because of their complex nature, cannot be expected to explain consumption adequately by themselves. While they may be somewhat dull, demographics are straightforward, concrete, and easily gathered. In this regard, demographics can identify potential customers and suggest ways to satisfy them more precisely.

TOTAL POPULATION AND AGE

Consumption is always related to population. In the most obvious way, when population declines, so does consumption. When it increases, the amount of consumption will expand accordingly. In the United States, the population grew from 76 million to 179 million, or about 136 percent, between 1900 and 1960. The population has grown steadily over those years and reached 234 million in 1985, up from 213 million in 1975.

In terms of households, the number topped 90 million for the first time in 1988, up from 80 million in 1980. The households are projected to reach 102 million in 2000. Yet it must be pointed out that household size has become smaller, from more than 4 persons per household in 1930 to 3.14 in 1970, 2.75 in 1985, and 2.64 in 1988. Still, the number of households is good news for marketers because more households means more purchases of appliances and other household items.

It is simply inadequate to observe total population trends without taking various subpopulations into account, since consumption varies greatly from one subpopulation to another. Several subpopulations can be identified on the basis of age, and the segment is important because these subpopulations do not grow at the same rate.

As can be seen from Exhibit 3.1, the number of households headed by those under 35 years old is projected to drop absolutely as well as relatively.[1] In contrast, the other two groups (the 35-to-49 and 50-plus age groups) are supposed to grow, with the households headed by people between 35 and 49 being the faster-growing of the two. This trend is significant because the 35-to-49 age group has a great deal of spending power due to peak income and the accumulation of wealth. By the year 2000, this group will have 120 million people or about 45 percent of the total population.

Another important group is the over-64 group. This segment has been growing steadily and will continue to do so because of the expanded life expectancy. The segment will increasingly gain membership in the second decade of the next century when babies born during the baby

Exhibit 3.1
Household Trends

	households (in millions)	
	1985	2000
less than 35 years old	25.5 (29%)	22.0 (22%)
35-49 age group	23.8 (27%)	35.0 (34%)
50+ age group	37.5 (43%)	45.5 (44%)
total U.S.	86.8 (100%)	102.5 (100%)

boom years become senior citizens. By 2025, one-fifth of all Americans will fall into this group.

Generally speaking, the trends indicate that between now and the turn of the century the number of Americans in their 20s will decline by 20 percent, while the number of those in their 40s and those over 85 will increase by one-half and two-thirds respectively. The change in each group would have special meaning for different industries since various age groups are heavy users of different products. Obviously, baby food companies depend on the 0–4 year olds. The heartiest candy eaters are the 5–17 age group. The lifeblood of the soft drink industry consists of those between the age of 13 and 24. The largest single group of smokers (34.7 percent of all smokers) is those between 18 and 24. For furniture, it is the 30- to 39-year-old age group which spends more money per capita on furniture than any other. On the other hand, amateur remodelers are mostly between 25 and 44, an attractive segment for a do-it-yourself market. In contrast, cigar smoking is more common with men over 55.

It should be pointed out that the U.S. population is getting older. With the median age under 28 in 1970, it reached 30 at around 1980 and will become 35 by the turn of the century. By 2020, almost one-third of the U.S. population (i.e., 94 million adults) will be 55 or older, making it an 81 percent increase from the 1988 figure. This trend will adversely affect consumption of soft drinks and purchases of records and fast foods. On the other hand, the soda-guzzling youth market will turn to harder beverages (i.e., liquor) as it matures. Likewise, such a trend is welcomed by cigar manufacturers and pharmaceutical producers, who will benefit from an aging population.

The graying of the U.S. population is expected to be accompanied by the growing mood of conservatism in attitudes and tastes as a result of the maturation of the population and the waning of the youth culture. Consequently, product obsolescence may slow down, while new products will not be easily accepted. These older customers will, because of their conservative tastes, demand quality, durability, and variety in future purchases.

While there is no doubt that the changing demographics will injure some companies, it does not mean that they are helpless. Actually, there are many things which can be undertaken to remedy any unfavorable trend as well as to take advantage of it. In the case of the soft drink industry, losses will be several million customers in the 13 to 24 age group who would have consumed some 3.3 billion cans of soft drinks since, on average, each youngster consumes 823 cans of soda pop annually. Because drinkers consume fewer soft drinks as they become older, it will be critical to develop brand loyalty to keep old customers. Furthermore, advertisements must be developed for older consumers, or an existing theme must be modified to include these older drinkers. For example, the "Pepsi Generation" must eventually include adult drinkers.

Also new products conforming to older consumers' tastes should be introduced. In this case, mature drinkers will demand more diet drinks and citrus-flavored drinks which can be used as mixers. Containers should be childproof but not seniorproof. Doors do not have to have knobs and can be replaced with latches. Appliances should have bigger buttons and better visual displays. Labels with big print and simpler operating instructions are desirable.

Recognizing the importance of the 52 million consumers who are older than 55 years old, the greeting card industry has begun to market cards designed exclusively for this group. American Greetings has made plans to offer "milestone birthdays" cards (e.g., 75th, 80th, etc.). Hallmark's effort, in contrast, is much more extensive. The company markets "the Best Years" product line consisting of 129 cards for senior citizens. Based on the results of marketing research, these cards offer humor and allow the over-55 card buyers to have fun by kidding each other about aging. There are also specialized cards for such occasions as the death of a pet and an extended vacation. Other cards can be sent to thank a care-giver (e.g., a nurse, a friend) or children for arranging the visit of grandchildren.

BIRTH RATE

The past half century has produced three drastic shifts in birth rate and subsequently in consumption. Initially, there was the "birth dearth" of the depression years with total births dropping from almost 3 million to 2.5 million annually. Then came the "baby boom" years of 1946–55, when the number of births surged past the 4 million mark for each year in that particular decade. That decade resulted in the only upturn in 170 years of otherwise declining fertility in the United States. The present time is the "baby bust" period with a progressively declining fertility rate which, in 1988, was at an all-time low—even far below the population replacement level. Because the average American woman will have only 1.8 children in her lifetime, the U.S. population will decline after 2030 despite immigration.[2]

The declining rate in the 1960s and early 1970s was a surprise, especially when demographers predicted an upturn when children born during the baby boom years reached the marriageable age. They failed, however, to note several important trends: (1) better family planning with more effective birth control methods, (2) couples' preference for paychecks over pregnancy, (3) trends toward smaller family size, childless couples, and single-person households, (4) falling marriage and rising divorce rates, (5) delayed marriage as well as deferred childbearing, (6) two-income families, (7) higher education levels, (8) women's greater experience and career opportunities, (9) urbanization, (10) legal abortion, and (11) high costs of rearing and educating children. These trends are positively related and tend to reinforce each other. Not surprisingly, they significantly and adversely affect baby food companies. Heinz has closed down one baby food plant, and its other two plants ran at only 75 percent capacity. For Gerber, its diversification in the late 1960s and 1970s away from the baby business has met with limited success.

Prospects are once again looking good for baby-product companies, in spite of other negative trends, primarily because of the number of women born during the baby boom years who are now in their childbearing years (15–44). Confronted with a now-or-never situation, many of them who have postponed childbearing are embarking on parenthood.

In addition to their interest in the birth rate increase, baby-oriented companies are also welcoming a sharp rise in the number of first births. Accounting for 38.4 percent of the total births in 1970, first births climbed to more than 40 percent in the 1980s. For marketers, such a prediction is important because, with first births, women are far more willing to buy all types of maternity goods ranging from children's foods to furniture needs. Since parenthood is now commonly planned, women are financially set to spend on pregnancy and can thus afford more and better clothing for this purpose. Many stores stock everything from blazers and suits to textured pantyhose and jogging suits as well as designer-name goods for expectant mothers.

WOMEN

Women, long overlooked and underestimated by marketers and researchers, are the population majority, accounting for over 51 percent of the total population. As a group, several characteristics should be noted. First, the female population has been aging, just like the total population, with the median age rising from 22.4 years at the turn of the century to about 30 at present. Second, the number of women of childbearing age (15 to 44) will increase by over 10 million between 1975 and 2000, a signal of a new baby boom period.

New Women: Working Women

The female labor force grew 123 percent between 1947 and 1975. As a percentage of the nation's labor force, women represented 29.6 percent of all workers in 1950. But their share has increased to 40 percent and may go as high as 51 percent by 1990, with more than half of all women over 15 years old in the labor force in 1985. In 1979, women's earnings were only 62 percent of men's, but the income gap has narrowed to 68 percent in 1986.

Wives in the labor force doubled between 1964 and 1984, from 13 million to 26 million or more than 60 percent of all working women, indicating a tendency for women to go back to work when children are in school. But why are women going back to work at such an unprecedented rate? The major causes are the rising cost of living and women's psychological satisfaction derived from working. Moreover, birth control, labor-saving devices, and the acceptance of the working-wife role all make it feasible and practical.

The impact of working women on the marketplace is obvious. Because of their contribution, families' total incomes have increased rapidly, resulting in more consumption generally. On a more specific level, the demand on women's time and energy further makes them receptive to products and services that are labor- and time-saving.

Working wives are not simply housewives who work. Both groups differ in many aspects across demographics, attitudes, lifestyles, and media and consumption habits. In terms of demographics, working women are younger, are generally more educated, and have higher family income levels.

With regard to lifestyle, working women are more likely to travel and stay in a hotel. They are more interested in themselves, self-improvement, and leisure. Emphasizing individualism, they are likely to be more independent and confident. While 60 percent of adult women agreed that "a woman's place is in the home" in 1967, only one quarter of them indicated that agreement a decade later. In contrast with traditional women, modern or working women are more cosmopolitan in their interests and more liberal in attitudes. Believing that homemaking is undervalued, they tend to avoid such tasks and transfer them to other people, for example, by eating more meals away from home. Related to their interest in personal appearance, physical conditioning, and leisure activities, they tend to read fashion-oriented and cosmopolitan magazines, which suggests one method of effectively reaching them.

Projected Trends

The world of the married working woman is constantly and rapidly changing. Some of the trends that have significant implications for business firms are that the working wife is seeking personal identity and individualism and that she accepts leisure time for pleasure and is concerned with convenience.

These trends, undoubtedly, will have significant impact on the methods of distribution for goods and services. Since modern working women find it difficult to shop during regular shopping hours or to wait at home during the day for appliance repairs, provisions for these services will increasingly be made available during evenings and weekends. Special promotional and sales events will also be scheduled at times more suitable for these women.

The importance of the women's market must be reassessed. It has been traditional to assume that financial matters—banking, insurance, and investment—are of concern only to men. As a result, financial institutions have concentrated their marketing efforts on reaching male customers. Financial institutions generally regarded women as nonpeople.[3] Fortunately, the situation has changed. Some financial institutions have begun to recognize the potential of the women's market and have begun to cultivate it.

Women and Advertising

Advertisers have long been criticized by minority groups such as blacks and working women on grounds that they are underused and not portrayed accurately in advertising. One study dealing with this criticism was conducted in 1970. Based on the content analysis of 729 advertisements in eight general-interest magazines such as *Life, Look, Newsweek*, the *New Yorker, Time, Saturday Review, U.S. News and World Report*, and *Reader's Digest*, the advertisements often employed the following cliches about women's roles: (1) a woman's place is in the home, (2) women do not make important decisions—they operate independently only for inexpensive products such as foods, cosmetics, and cleaning products, but men must be brought into the advertisements for expensive products supposedly to share decisions, (3) women are dependent on men's protection and approval for some social activities such as smoking, and (4) men regard women primarily as sexual objects instead of as people, as illustrated by women's decorative roles for many products.

Along the same line, another study indicated that there was a marked improvement in the number of working women portrayed in 1972 without any significant change in the frequency with which women were shown to operate independently of men when purchasing big-ticket items or when participating in institutional transactions with banks, industries, or mass media. It seems clear that, despite a marked improvement in the status of women over the years, women were still shown as unemployed persons or as low-income wage earners. In this regard, advertisements have been slow in recognizing the wide variety of roles women play in today's world.

Marketers have now begun to recognize the changing role of women, at least as far as TV commercials are concerned. There is considerable evidence of improvement in role portrayals of women.[4] In many instances, the difference in role portrayal between male and female characters was significantly less. Furthermore, female characters have moved closer to their actual roles.

While women may have been underrepresented and portrayed in unrealistic settings, the important question is whether product desirability will be enhanced if women are portrayed in a career or neutral (less traditional) role instead of in a sex-object, family, or fashion-object (more traditional) role. The answer must depend on specific products investigated. According to one study, for personal and grooming products, the desirability of such products is enhanced by career and neutral roles.[5] For other products such as those used in a household or family settings, the more traditional roles are preferred, regardless of whether female viewers agree with the tenets of the women's liberation movement or not. Thus, preference for specific female roles does not stay constant across product categories. Women recognize their many roles and will react primarily to product-use situations.

When it is appropriate for advertisers to break away from traditional stereotypes, three strategies are available: dual roles, role switching, and role blending.[6] With dual roles, women are shown to assume both traditional and nontraditional roles (e.g., a female tennis pro chooses certain beverages for her family). Role switching, on the other hand, employs women to use products traditionally associated with men (e.g., a woman is shown changing motor oil or painting and repairing furniture). In the case of role blending, neither sex is portrayed as dominating the purchase, implying joint decision. As shown in one Allstate commercial, neither the wife nor her husband knows much about home-owner's insurance, making it necessary for both to search for information together.

As a group, women are far from being homogeneous, and it is inappropriate to label them as working or nonworking. Some kind of segmentation by age, occupation, or attitude must be made to determine the appropriateness of roles to be used in advertisements. As shown in a study involving food preparation, the traditional woman wants high-quality food at a reasonable cost, without much concern about the shopping and meal preparation time.[7] The contemporary woman, in contrast, is concerned with time and is likely to use point-of-purchase information primarily to save time. The anticooking woman is attracted by a section within the promotion devoted to quickly prepared foods and quick checkout services. Therefore, women's atttitudes toward food preparation can be used to predict food shopping behavior and can suggest appropriate advertising appeals. These appeals, however, should be independent of women's work orientation.

Marketers must recognize that most women hold a multidimensional view of their world and their various roles within it. Instead of showing a working woman in a time-saving situation, advertisements should reflect the fact that the contemporary woman has multiple demands on her limited time. In any case, the implication is that for many products, advertisements should take into account new trends and freedoms now enjoyed by women. Virginia Slims, the number one cigarette for women, has done well due to the recognition of these trends.

Emotion vs. Caution

The female market, without doubt, is very attractive to marketers, and more products and media are now aimed at women than ever before. In addition to women's magazines, which have existed for many years, there is a female radio station (reflected even in its name, WOMN) in New Haven that broadcasts music, news, and commentary on both women's issues and general-interest issues as they affect women. Playing mostly soft rock and conservative contemporary music, the station makes certain that it does not play any music containing lyrics offensive to women, and female commentators are generally used.

There is, of course, a danger that the female appeal may go too far. Some caution must be exercised, since the female segment is still a relatively new market surrounded by uncertainty, optimism, and risks. Such is the case within the banking industry. Several women's banks, primarily owned and managed by women, seek to appeal mainly to women, in effect alienating male customers. These banks forget the fact that, while 60 percent of their customers are women, 70 percent of their deposit dollars come from men who hesitate to use their checks with the word "Women" on them. In the case of San Diego's Women's Bank, the name was finally changed to California Coastal Bank after the original name was found to be a deterrent to business. For other banks, difficulties have been experienced in making loans to customers simply because they are identified as "female" banks. The implication is that sound business practices must not be replaced by militant feminism or emotions. The potential and size of each market segment must be assessed carefully, and each transaction must be evaluated on its own merits.

INCOME

Income is one of the most often used variables in predicting consumption. There are, however, several kinds of income. They do not predict expenditures with the same accuracy. It is then useful to distinguish the different kinds of income.

Types of Income

There are at least three kinds of income: personal, disposable, and discretionary. *Personal income* is the total income from all sources regardless of whether they are taxable. These sources include wages, salaries, dividends, interest, social security, pensions, profit sharing, capital gains, and rent receipts. As far as the Internal Revenue Service is concerned, personal income is the most interesting category of income.

Based on a ranking of 317 metropolitan areas by the Department of Commerce, the five richest metropolitan areas and their average per capita personal incomes are Bridgeport-Stamford-Norwalk, Connecticut ($24,501), San Francisco ($23,542), Bergen-Passaic, New Jersey ($21,518), Middlesex-Somerset-Hunterdon, New Jersey ($21,142), and San Jose, California ($20,935). The poorest five are El Paso, Texas ($9,177), Provo-Orem, Utah ($8,528), Brownsville-Harlingen, Texas ($7,205), Laredo, Texas ($6,850), and McAllen-Edinburg-Mission, Texas ($6,800). Of the top 15, 13 of them are in California, Florida, or the Northeast, while the 15 poorest are all in the Southeast and Southwest. It is important to note that rich areas tend to get richer as shown by the evidence that approximately two-thirds of the richest 106 metropolitan areas had faster-than-average income growth in 1986 while less than one-third of the 105 poorest areas had that experience. Not surprisingly, the top-vs.-bottom difference has moved from $14,920 in 1984 to $17,701 in 1986, indicating a widening gap.

Disposable income is the amount of personal income less taxes. But what kind of taxes are there? In certain parts of Pennsylvania, a resident would pay all of the following taxes: federal income tax, state income tax, county income tax, city income tax, occupation privilege tax, property tax, and school tax. In other words, disposable income is the amount of money available for personal consumption and saving after all taxes have been paid.

Discretionary income is the disposable income less necessary living costs and fixed commitments. Examples of some of these costs and fixed commitments include food, clothing, household utilities, transportation, rent, house mortgage payments, insurance, installment payments, and the like.

According to Runzheimer International in Rochester, Wisconsin, New York is the city with the highest cost of living, followed by San Jose, Santa Barbara, Boston, San Francisco, Honolulu, and Washington. In contrast, the least costly is Springfield (Missouri), followed by Canton (Ohio), Cheyenne (Wyoming), and Sioux Falls (South Dakota).

Engel's Law

As might be expected, income and consumption are positively related. As income rises, *absolute* expenditures for most products increase accordingly, except for *inferior* goods such as potatoes, pork and beans, and so forth. For these few products, consumption actually declines as income goes up, since they are regarded as foods consumed by the poor. But for typically normal goods, expenditures will increase in absolute terms. Relatively, however, consumption does not increase for all products. The explanation for the changes in expenditures for certain goods, as income changes, is found in Engel's law.

Established in 1848, Engel's law proposes a stable relationship between income and relative expenditures. According to this law, relative expenditures do not always go up with a rise in income. As a percentage or proportion of income, relative spending will go up for some products, remain stable for others, and decline for other categories of products. As income increases, the percentage spent will decline for food, remain stable for housing, and increase for clothing, transportation, recreation, health, and education. Part of the explanation for this is that poor families spend the largest proportion of income for essentials. As income increases, they eat more and better, but the percentage spent actually declines, leaving a larger proportion for discretionary items such as luxuries and savings.

How valid is Engel's law? According to one study conducted over the years between 1929 and 1953, the law holds true only 45 percent of the time. Evidently income by itself is not adequate to predict purchases. As stated earlier, there are three types of income which can yield varying results in prediction. Furthermore, the amount of income by itself can be a misleading indicator of wealth. It is erroneous, for example, to use income as a measure of wealth, because wealth can also be expressed in terms of possessions. For the inividual with a low income due to recent retirement, it may still be possible to continue spending as before retirement if a large savings account and other valuable possessions are held.

In order to understand consumer expenditure in this case, income must be supplemented by what is owned (i.e., household and financial assets that can be quickly converted into cash) as well as what can be borrowed (i.e., consumer credit granted by banks and credit card companies, among others). Home-equity loans, for instance, provide homeowners with $75 billion that they can borrow and spend. Or take the case of Sears's marketing of the Discover credit card. If Discover has ten million cardholders (or just about 20 percent of the Sears cardholders), each with a credit line of a few thousand dollars, Sears in effect has made it possible for consumers to acquire potential debt of some $20 billion and to use it for purchases and consumption.

The relationship between income and expenditures can be altered by the consumer's future expectation regarding his income and economy. If he is optimistic about his future potential earnings, he may decide to purchase durables immediately. For example, a worker expecting a big pay increase or a graduating college student who has accepted an attractive job offer may go ahead with an automobile purchase immediately. Conversely, when the consumer's future expectation is unfavorable, his pessimism may force him to postpone the purchase. Such was the case with automobile sales in the summer of 1979. High gas prices and shortages, rapid inflation, and consumers' lack of confidence in the economy were the major causes of excessive, unsold automobile inventories.

The relationship between demand and income is further complicated by the fact that pessimism sometimes spurs sales instead of slowing them down. In spite of so many negative signs about the nation's economy in 1978 and 1979, consumers actually stepped up their spending on many big-ticket items, ranging from durables to quality silverware and jewelry. This peculiar phenomenon can be attributed to the buy-in-advance psychology. Expecting that prices in all likelihood will only go up, consumers purchase quality products as a hedge against inflation. Their rationale: the only way to save money is to spend it as soon as possible because money will become worth less in the future.

During that period, in their effort to overcome inflation, consumers took on new debt at a rate of 50 percent faster than the increase in their income. Consequently, the nation's total consumer debt at the time stood at $1 trillion or $4,600 for every person in the country. After taxes, another 21 cents of each dollar had to go to pay off the existing debt, an unprecedented burden on the consumer.

In the late 1980s, economists repeatedly predicted that the economy was going to slow down. Yet the economy continued to be strong, defying experts' forecasts. Consumer spending and consumer debt continued to grow. Given this situation, it is obvious that consumers are the ones carrying the economy.

The danger of the above practice is that consumers can only keep their heads above water if the economy stays in high gear. If it ever slows down, even temporarily, consumers will stop spending, aggravating the recession even more, because a larger share of their income then must be allocated for the higher prices of food and nondurables. Just like in 1974 when a great deal of credit buying and high interest rates developed, credit became unavailable or too expensive and without warning, buying suddenly stopped. At present, the ratio of consumer installment debt to disposable income is almost 20 percent, a record and precarious level.

What are the implications for business firms when the income variable within a demography is affected in this way? It means that manufacturers and retailers must be extremely cautious with their inventories under the conditions of high inflation, high interest rates, and excessive credit buying. To cut down on inventory while consumers continue spending will result in shortages and, subsequently, lost sales and profits. On the other hand, too high an inventory level will generate heavy financing costs when credit-laden consumers stop buying. Naturally, when stuck with high inventories, retailers will stop further purchases, and manufacturers will stop producing, resulting in further layoffs and a worsening of the recession. Fortunately, most business firms seemed to have learned a lesson from 1974. They now watch their inventories very carefully and are in a better position to cope with recession instead of aggravating it as happened in the past.

Two-Income Family

As stated earlier, an unprecedented number of working wives are now a part of the labor force. Of the 85 million households in 1985, one-third is represented by two-income families. Because of the career-oriented wife, a large number of families will find themselves in the middle- and upper-income brackets. For marketers, the realization should be that the two-income family spends more money and spends it differently—differently from a family whose equivalent income is derived from a single source. For example, a typical dual-income couple employs more household help but does less home entertainment. Such a trend, if continued, will of course adversely affect supermarkets and liquor stores. Furthermore, the size of the affluent, dual-income families understates the importance of such families, since they account for half of expenditures on such products as clothes, power tools, dishwashers, microwave ovens, and leisure products.

In general, the consumer market does look attractive for marketers because consumers' discretionary income will rise. But in what markets will this increase in income be spent? Demographic trends suggest a strong demand for household durables, textiles, do-it-yourself products, entertainment, travel, recreation, adult education, and convenience- and experience-oriented goods and services for the future.

Inflation tends to encourage leisure-time activities at home and is also likely to shrink the size of new homes. To accommodate such a change in homes, furniture will have to be more compact and serve multi-purpose functions such as convertible sofas and reclining chairs. Homes, it is expected, will also be better insulated and equipped with multiple-use functions.

With less time for shopping, the dual income family will be interested in time-saving services. Mail order houses and catalog showrooms are likely to flourish and to gain larger retail market share. These outlets will probably stock the more familiar brands as consumers will not have time to experiment with less familiar brands and products.

GEOGRAPHIC LOCATION

Geographic location, it has been found, has an effect on market demand in three different ways: (1) geographic density, (2) geographic mobility, and (3) geographic customs and patterns. Each of these three aspects of geographic location along with their market implications is discussed below.

Geographic Density

Perhaps the most obvious effect of geographic location is expressed in terms of its density. Density and total demand are related in that the greater the density, the greater consumption will be. In this regard, however, density does not exactly explain consumption variation among products or groups of people—just the aggregate amount of consumption. For business firms, the implication that is suggested is that the area of market interest must be sufficiently populated to justify a market operation. As a rule of thumb, for example, many fast-food establishments will not open a store in a city of less than 100,000 population.

While total population has been increasing, the growth patterns may vary from one part of the country to another. In New England, North

Central, and the Southern states along the eastern seaboard, the population has been increasing in the absolute terms. In relative terms, however, the proportion or percentage of the nation's population these regions represent has actually been on the decline. For some regions, such as the city of St. Louis, the population has declined both absolutely and relatively. The substantial growth regions, on the other hand, have been the West, South Central, Mountain, and Pacific states.

Between 1986 and 2000, it is expected that the U.S. population will increase by 26.6 million people. The top 40 metropolitan areas will account for half of this growth. According to NPA Data Services Inc., the top 10 metropolitan areas and the increases expected for these areas by the year 2000 are as follows: Los Angeles (1,017,000), Houston (791,000), Riverside (724,000), Atlanta (617,000), Phoenix (594,000), Dallas (576,000), Anaheim (567,000), San Diego (558,000), Washington (550,000), and Tampa (473,000).

Marketers should recognize the regional shifts in population in order to determine whether market services should be increased or reduced. At the present time, the largest markets are still in the East and these account for roughly 40 percent of total consumption. Some experts believe that Los Angeles may someday replace New York as the largest city. This is not an unreasonable projection given the fact that Los Angeles has gained the most people in the 1980s.

In the United States, three distinct phases of population movement have been observed: (1) the growth of metropolises, (2) the growth of suburbia, and (3) the growth of megalopolises. These three phases are somewhat related, and a brief discussion of each stage is provided below.

The Growth of Metropolises. The first significant shift within the population occurred as a result of the movement of the population from rural to urban areas, with the result that many metropolitan areas experienced significant increases in population. Although the trend has slowed, metropolitan areas are still gaining population. Between 1983 and 1984, metropolitan areas gained 2.6 million people while losing 2.3 million.

Given these changes, marketing activities must be adjusted to meet varying needs of residents. When the population becomes densely concentrated, the competition among businesses in a big city is very intense in terms of price and shopping hours. The density of population also justifies the existence of specialized establishments such as museums, Chinatown, and professional sports. In other words, a wide range of commercial and cultural activities can be offered due to the geographic concentration of the population. Marketers are also benefited and find it easy to get in touch with their customers because of the availability of all kinds of advertising media, ranging from local TV stations to local magazines. Chicago, for example, has such magazines as *Chicago* and *Chicago Times*.

In small towns, on the other hand, marketers cannot be very selective because there may be no local TV station or local magazines. It is also not uncommon for these small towns to have no newspaper or to have a newspaper which is only published once or twice a week.

The Growth of Suburbia. The second major shift in population occurs when the movement is from central cities to suburbs. High city taxes, traffic congestion, downtown deterioration, and pollution are some of the primary casues for this movement. Compared with a 1 percent incrase in population for central cities during the 1960s, the suburbs experienced a growth of over 25 percent. The recent growth of metropolitan areas was due to the gains made by suburbs rather than by central cities. Between 1983 and 1984, 5.5 million people moved from nonsuburbs to suburbs, with only 3.5 million Americans moving the other way. In contrast, central cities lost 5.1 million people while gaining only 3.3 million people. Not surprisingly, half of the entire U.S. population is suburban.

From their modest start as a small satellite of the center city, suburban communities have grown into marketing entities of their own. Many suburban communities now have large commercial buildings and planned shopping centers. In effect, they have become independent of the core city, and suburbanites no longer have to travel to the central city area for shopping or to go to work.

In response to this population shift, many metropolitan newspapers such as the *Washington Post* offer special suburban editions. These special suburban editions, however, may not be market efficient. When compared with a surburban press which reaches 80 percent of suburban homes, most central city dailies have an average suburban household coverage of less than 50 percent. A typical suburban household is a family with a white-collar household head. These families shop locally even when they see advertisements in metropolitan papers. What this means is that suburbia has its own lifestyle that is not strongly influenced by the attractions of the core city and that suburbia should be considered as a distinct market.

The Growth of Megalopolises. In many parts of the country, the metropolitan areas have expanded to the point where there remains no rural space among them. The joining and blending together of metropolitan areas becomes known as a megalopolis or interurbia.

The largest and best known megalopolis is found along the Atlantic coastline, where there is virtually no space between the standard metropolitan areas beginning at Boston and going on to New York, Philadelphia, Baltimore, Washington, D.C., and ending at Norfolk, Virginia.

Another well-known megalopolis occurs on the shores of the Great Lakes and across the lower part of Michigan; it includes the cities of Buffalo, Detroit, Gary, Chicago, and Milwaukee.

What are the important business and marketing implications of megalopolises? Megalopolises are likely to have the following impact upon marketing and business activity.

Heavy and concentrated consumption occurs in a megalopolis. For example, the Atlantic coastline can be considered a 600-mile-long market, comprised of less than 2 percent of the nation's land but representing 24 percent of all retail sales. For all interurbias combined, the figures show that more than half of the nation's retail sales and almost half of the total population are to be found within these regions. With an average of 620 people per square mile, or 12 times as many people as the rest of the country, these interurbias account for a substantial portion of all business activity across the United States.

Consumers in megalopolises are relatively liberal and are likely to be product innovators. These interurbian men and women are also above the national average in their desire for achievement and are likely to hold professional leadership positions in business. Interurbian dwellers are more likely to try new products because of: (1) liberal attitudes, (2) preference for variety and novelty, and (3) higher incomes, enabling them to afford the rather high prices charged in these markets. Given this purchase behavior, marketers should introduce new products in the interurbian markets, because interurbian consumers are more likely to respond to them and will help determine whether these new luxuries will become necessities.

Geographic Mobility

The United States is characterized by a willingness toward geographic mobility within its population. The average American will move at least eleven times in his lifetime. This unique characteristic offers companies a basis on which to segment their markets and to identify distinct groups of target markets with special needs. The mobile segment is important because of its size and represents about 17 percent of the population making residential changes each year. Of course, the percentage varies from region to region. In the Washington, D.C., area, for example, the proportion may go as high as one-third because of a large number of federal government employees.

Geographic mobility among individuals is a function of a set of external and internal conditions that occur within the individual's environment. External factors are basically concerned with the availability of job opportunities. In contrast, internal factors are psychological variables which dictate the individual's willingness to move. These psychological factors include attitudes toward risk and changes.

Some of the characteristics common among geographic mobiles should be noted. They tend to be younger, and those in their 20s and early 30s move the most.[8] The median age of people who made five or more moves in three years was 24 as compared with 48 for nonmovers. Movers have fewer children and have a higher level of education attainment. In comparison with settled residents, movers also have higher incomes and asset levels which are likely derived from the concentration of managerial, technical, and professional occupations as well as the mobiles' higher aspiration levels.

Most movers do not move far. Of the 39 million movers between 1983–84, only 3.5 million moved to a different region. An overwhelming majority, 24 million or 62 percent, moved locally within their county. Long-distance movers are better educated than their short-distance counterparts.

Because of some of these unique characteristics, mobiles have special needs of which marketers should be aware. Their lifestyles demand products and services such as furniture, clothing, drapes, appliances, automobiles, housesitters, relocation services, moving and storage services, real estate services, and rental services for items such as furniture and trucks. As might be expected, movers are not especially brand loyal, and brand switching is common when they arrive in the new environment.

For the mobile segment to be a meaningful market, geographic mobiles must be reached with efficiency. This does not pose any special problems, since more than half of them read two or more newspapers daily. Also there are magazines such as *Changing Homes* and *New Home* that are designed especially for recent movers. Furthermore, business can even achieve a degree of selectivity by obtaining a list of new movers from utility and telephone companies. Insurance companies may want to get in touch with the new residents through the use of direct mail by obtaining new residents' names from banks or savings and loan associations where new movers are likely to open new accounts or may apply for home-mortgage loans.

Geographic mobility, a uniquely American characteristic, is now slowing down, having declined from the all-time high of 21 percent of the population between 1960–61 to 17 percent of the population annually. Several factors appear to contribute to this decline: dual-career marriages, a rising average age of the population, high costs of moving, emphasis on leisure activities, teleconferencing, and many companies' recent discontinuance of mobility as a basis for promotion.[9]

Mobility is on the rise again. After bottoming out at 16.6 percent in 1983, the mobility rate has climbed steadily back up to more than 17 percent. It is also interesting to note that the 200-year trend of farm to city migration has recently been reversed. For the first decade in history, beginning in the 1970s, people are now moving back to rural areas to settle in small towns due to the lower cost of living, better air quality, and more attractive environment. As mobility declines and as small towns grow, jobs will have to move to people. As a result, teleconferencing and telemarketing may be the future means of communication with consumers. A surge in retail sales in small towns can also be expected, and small-town discounters such as Wal-Mart will substantially benefit from the anticipated rural movement of the population.

Geographic Customs

In much the same way as climate and length of season, consumption patterns among consumers vary from one region to another. Demand for many products is dictated by a given area's climate and customs. For example, soft drinks and beer are consumed more in the warm climate areas, while coffee and hot chocolate are consumed more in the cold regions. In Houston, often called the air-conditioned capital of the world, air-conditioning along with high electricity consumption is a way of life because of the humidity. In contrast, the northern states require more home heating fuel, skis, and snowmobiles. Even color preference is affected by geographic region: cooler colors for the North, and brighter colors in the South.

The nation's five geographic regions and the descriptions of the people in these areas are: East (cosmopolitan travelers), South (political conservatives), Midwest (average or typical Americans), Southwest (traditionalists), and West (liberals).[10] These regions' consumption and media patterns greatly vary. For example, those in the East enjoy cocktails before dinner and are most likely to read evening newspapers. Southerners, on the other hand, have a preference for country and western music. Westerners, in contrast, like neither country and western music nor evening newspapers but are most likely to buy vitamin tablets, yogurt, and domestic wine and to go out for breakfast.

Acknowledging market diversity, Campbell Soup Co. has led the charge toward regional marketing.[11] To move marketing decision making out of corporate headquarters and into the field, the company appointed a brand sales manager for each of the 22 sales regions to: (1) tailor national efforts, (2) arrange regional promotions, and (3) research local trends. A result of this move is new products which conform to regional styles and tastes. For example, Campbell came up with the idea of canned nacho cheese sauce which, once heated, could be poured over nacho chips. The pilot version proved to be too hot for the eastern United States but not hot enough for the West and Southwest. Instead of using the traditional approach of going right down the middle for something which is "just about right" (but not quite right) for everyone, Campbell decided to have a hot version for the West and Southwest and a milder cheese sauce for other regions.

Naturally, regional marketing is less efficient than national marketing. However, the extra costs are offset by the increase in competitiveness and flexibility. By acting local, a mature or declining market can still offer growth potential.

CONCLUSION

Demographics are important because they offer a reliable way of understanding consumer behavior. Since consumers' demographic characteristics are continually changing, marketers should carefully observe trends in such characteristics as birth rate, age mix, sex, income, and geographic distribution.

While birth rates were on a decline in the 1970s, total births are now beginning to pick up again, and this is undoubtedly welcome news for baby-oriented companies. Not all segments of the market, however, grow at the same pace. As a matter of fact, some market segments may even be in decline. Such is the case at present with the youth market. In contrast, however, the adult and senior-citizen segments are expected to grow rapidly in the near future.

Working women are also contributing to the market significantly as their working habits become more and more accepted within society. After so many years of stereotyping women in advertisements, marketers are finally recognizing their new lifestyle and their working role in society. Advertisers must, however, continue to be careful and realize that there is no specific role among women which is appropriate for all products.

The chapter also examines the various types of income as well as the relationship between income and Engel's law. The findings at the present time are that the relationship between income and expenditures can be moderated by intervening variables such as psychological factors. The uncertainty within the economy and high inflation in the marketplace, however, do make it necessary to examine carefully the relationship between income and expenditures.

Marketers should pay close attention to geographic location and its three important aspects of density, mobility, and customs. Total consumption is affected by population density, while patterns of consumption may vary among regions because of local customs and preferences. On the other hand, geographic mobility offers marketers a unique market which is interested in several kinds of particular offerings and which can be reached with a distinct marketing mix.

NOTES

1. Fabian Linden, "Middle-Aged Muscle," *American Demographics*, October 1987, p. 4.

2. Ben J. Wattenberg, *The Birth Dearth* (New York: Pharos Books, 1987).

3. Rena Bartos, *The Moving Target* (New York: Free Press, 1982).

4. Kenneth C. Schneider and Sharon Barich Schneider, "Trends in Sex Roles in Television Commercials," *Journal of Marketing* 43 (Summer 1979): 79–84.

5. Lawrence H. Wortzel and John M. Frisbie, "Women's Role Portrayal Preferences in Advertisements: An Empirical Study," *Journal of Marketing* 38 (October 1974): 41–46.

6. William J. Lundstrom and Donald Sciglimpaglia, "Sex Role Portrayals in Advertising," *Journal of Marketing* 41 (July 1977): 72–79.

7. May Lou Roberts and Lawrence H. Wortzel, "New Life-Style Determinants of Women's Food Shopping Behavior," *Journal of Marketing* 43 (Summer 1979): 28–39.

8. Bureau of Census, *Geographical Mobility March 1983 to March 1984*, Current Population Reports, Series P–20, No. 407, 1986; William Dunn, "Americans on the Move," *American Demographics*. October 1986, pp. 49–51, 73; Joe Schwartz, "On the Road Again," *American Demographics*, April 1987, pp. 39–42.

9. "America's New Immobile Society," *Business Week*, 27 July 1981, pp. 58–62.

10. Fred D. Reynolds and William D. Wells, *Consumer Behavior* (New York: McGraw-Hill, 1977), pp. 207–15.

11. Larry Carpenter, "How to Market to Regions," *American Demographics*, November 1987, pp. 44–45; "Marketing's New Look," *Business Week*, 26 January 1987, pp. 64–69.

4

Diffusion of Innovations

THE DIFFUSION PROCESS OF INNOVATIONS

Invention is the creation of something new. But this something new is relatively useless to consumers unless marketers are willing to assume risks in introducing the new item. The introduction of something new is *innovation*. Gatorade was invented by a medical professor in 1965 for the University of Florida's football team. The drink, a solution of salt, water, and glucose, was designed to be absorbed quickly by the body to replace fluids lost during strenuous physical activity. The taste of the product, however, left much to be desired. Two years later, Stokely bought the rights to the product and, after making the taste more acceptable, introduced it to the market.

Marketers, preferring to minimize risks, will find it advantageous to understand how an innovation is diffused. The best way to understand the diffusion process is to begin by examining its definition. The diffusion process of innovations is (1) the adoption (2) over time (3) of new products or services (4) by adopting units (5) within social systems (6) in a given culture (7) as stimulated by marketing activities. Each component of the definition needs explanation and is discussed below.

Adoption should not be considered the equivalent of a trial purchase. A one-time purchase is not an adoption, but continued purchases do constitute an adoption. A consumer's adoption involves the conviction that the purchased product is desirable, and this conviction involves an acceptance or commitment on the part of the consumer as related to the product.

All consumers do not purchase a new product at the same *time*. Innovator consumers thus can be distinguished from other groups of adopters based on the time they enter the market. The time of entry element makes it possible to determine the proportionate size of each of the adopter groups and to gauge the extent of success of an innovation.

An item which is being adopted may be an idea, service, or object. In the marketing context, an adoption involves *new products or services*. What is "new," however, is subject to a number of interpretations. Newness can be narrowly or broadly defined, and it can also be objectively or subjectively defined.

The narrow definition of an innovation is based on a time restriction that is placed on the period that a product can be considered new. That is, only products which have recently been made available in the market are new. The broad definition, on the other hand, does not have a time constraint, since this definition is primarily concerned with consumer perception. In this regard, any product is new as long as it is perceived so by consumers, regardless of the interval of time since its introduction.

A subjective definition, which is based on consumer perception, is also provided. According to this definition, a product is considered new as long as the consumer views it as being different from other product classes or forms regardless of whether the perceived difference is real or imaginary. Whereas the subjective definition allows a product to be defined as new simply because of a successful marketing campaign, the objective definition is much more restrictive. In this case, a product can be new only when it is "quantitatively" different from other existing products. Therefore, a new package or image change is not adequate to make the claim that the product is new, even though consumers may be led to believe so.

As far as the Federal Trade Commission is concerned, only the narrow and objective definition should be used. For a product to be new, it must be "either entirely new or changed in a functionally significant and substantial respect." Furthermore, the FTC states that a product should not be described as new after the product has been in regular distribution for a period of six months.

For our purposes, the definition used in this book is a flexible one. It includes a totally new product, an old product in a new geographic area, a slightly modified product, an old product with a new package, and so on.

An *adopting unit* can be an individual or a group of individuals. The members of the group may be related as in the case of a family, or they may not be related to each other at all as in the case of a group of high school students. The term also includes commercial and industrial users regardless of whether or not they are profit-seeking entities.

A diffusion cannot exist outside of a *social system*. If an individual who is isolated adopts a product, this adoption is not considered part of the diffusion process since the individual has no relation to or impact on other people. Therefore, a proper requisite of a diffusion is that it must take place within a social structure. This social structure may be as broad as the entire U.S. population or as small as a family.

The diffusion process will vary from *culture* to culture. Culture exerts a great deal of influence on whether a new product is suitable and whether it should be accepted. Therefore, a product highly appropriate and accepted in one culture may be totally unsuitable and unacceptable elsewhere.

In general, the diffusion of a new product does not proceed on its own but is encouraged by *marketing activities*. Such activities essentially consist of the four Ps of marketing: product, price, place (distribution), and promotion. All of these controllable variables making up the marketing mix are used by marketers to communicate with and to influence consumers.

CLASSIFICATION OF INNOVATIONS

Innovations can be described based upon the disrupting effect an innovation has on established consumer habits. Based on this consideration, there are three categories of innovations: (1) continuous, (2) dynamically continuous, and (3) discontinuous innovations. A continuous innovation is defined as least likely to disrupt existing consumption patterns since it involves a relatively minor, cosmetic change in the product (e.g., styling). More disrupting effects are caused by a product which is considered a dynamically continuous innovation, because the changes in the product that are affected are more functionally and engineering related. Finally, a discontinuous innovation is a completely new product which performs a completely new function, resulting in the development of new use consumption patterns within the consumer.

It is not an easy task to categorize innovations. When a product is significantly modified, it is often not clear whether it should be considered a continuous extension of an existing diffusion (i.e., product class) or whether it is the beginning of a new diffusion (i.e., product form) altogether. The VCR market serves as a good illustration. Sony founded the consumer VCR market when it introduced its Betamax, with its three-hour recording time. Soon after, Panasonic entered the market with the VHS system, offering a four-hour recording time. Subsequent VHS units lengthened the recording time to six hours and finally to eight hours. The next generation of VCRs may switch from a 1/2-inch tape format to 1/4-inch. In each of these instances, is the technology evolutionary or revolutionary? Without the *operational* definition of a continuous, dynamically continuous, and discontinuous innovation, the determination (or measurement) of the type of innovation under consideration is very difficult.

Any classification system which is developed and used should function as a means to an end and not an end in itself. A good classification scheme thus must serve some useful purpose. Unfortunately, none of the three innovation categories as defined suggests an appropriate marketing strategy.

To remedy the situation, perhaps innovations should be related to the extent of marketing effort required to overcome varying degrees of consumer resistance. The impact of innovations on existing products should also be considered. When considered in this regard, all innovations can be placed on a continuous scale ranging from replacement innovation at one end to complementary innovation at the other. It should also be noted that most discontinuous innovations (e.g., computers and VCRs), will gradually move to the opposite (continuous innovation) end of the scale as time progresses.

Products such as the automobile and refrigerator, for example, were replacement innovations when they were first introduced since they were intended to replace trains (or horse-drawn carriages) and iceboxes respectively. Replacements are generally radical and will encounter strong opposition from industries being replaced. Likewise, consumers also offer resistance because their existing products are being made obsolete and because new products alter their habits and attitudes. Normally, the acceptance of new products is delayed until consumers need (*not* want) to replace products they currently own.

Complementary innovations, in contrast, do not replace existing products. Complementary innovations are designed so that consumers can get more out of existing products. The video cassette recorder, for example, is a complementary innovation. It does not replace television, but instead it enables viewers to get more out of their television sets by recording selected programs. Consumer opposition to complementary innovations is not usually strong because the extent of attitude change is relatively small. Consumers are likely to adopt complementary innovations as soon as their discretionary incomes permit them to do so.

But with replacement innovations, consumers are slower in their adoption regardless of their financial condition, and often wait until existing products they own no longer work satisfactorily. The reason that new methods of heating homes (i.e., more efficient heaters) are slow in gaining acceptance is because they are semireplacement innovations in the sense that homeowners must replace or significantly modify their existing home-heating systems when the new systems are installed. Therefore, consumers prefer to wait until their existing system must be replaced or until they buy a new home.

DIFFUSION AND PRODUCT-LIFE-CYCLE CURVES

Innovators are always the first but not the only group of consumers to adopt a new product or service. In addition to innovators, there are four other groups of consumers who also adopt the same product, but at a later time. As can be seen in Figure 4.1, based on the time of adoption, the other adopter groups are identified as early adopters, early majority, late majority, and laggards. Normally, the proportion of consumers within each group will vary according to the product category.

The patterns of acceptance for many products indicate that diffusion curves are bell shaped and that adoption tends to be normally distributed as shown in Exhibit 4.1. Exhibit 4.2 provides the same kind of information, except that this curve provides the information in a cumulative form.

It should be readily apparent that the cumulative adoption curve highly resembles the product-life-cycle curve. The basic difference between the two curves is that product life cycle is concerned with sales levels (units or dollars) and market characteristics whereas the diffusion process focuses on the number of adopters (percent) and their characteristics over the same time period.

The cumulative diffusion curve with its upward direction curve ap-

Exhibit 4.1
Noncumulative Adoption Curve

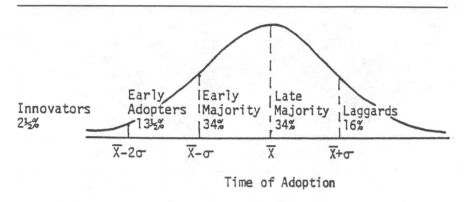

Time of Adoption

Exhibit 4.2
Cumulative Adoption Curves

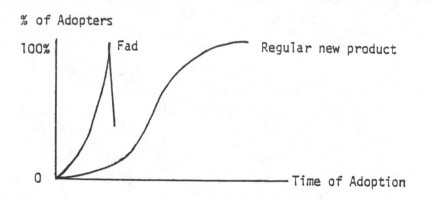

proaching 100 percent diffusion over time and the noncumulative, bell-shaped curve encompassing all 100 percent of adopters are quite misleading because: (1) there are always some consumers who resist a new product, (2) the population tends to grow over time, (3) population replacement should be taken into account because the population is not static—some individuals will leave the target population and be replaced by others, and (4) the cumulative adoption curve is likely to shift downward in the later stages because the product will be upgraded or replaced by a new competitive innovation. Therefore, even if the time of adoption is indefinite, the complete adoption of a new product by the total population is extremely unlikely.

If the portrayal of the cumulative diffusion curve (showing its 100 percent adoption) is based on the number of consumers already having adopted the product (rather than the total market of all potential adopters). The curve still gives a very misleading picture, because the diffusion is seldom both complete and total, especially if products are still in the market. It is also unwise to accept the curve at face value, because the curve should be constantly upgraded due to adopters continually leaving or entering the market. Furthermore, if the adoption is considered at any point in time, whether for one month or one year, the number of adopters at that point must always equal and be considered to be 100 percent of adopters. Yet the curve based on one month of adoption and that based on one year of adoption will appear different even though both points actually represent 100 percent. Therefore, the cumulative curve should depict the number of adopters on an absolute rather than relative basis (i.e., percent) in order to properly illustrate the adoption process in the correct perspective.

The diffusion theory also fails to note and discuss that many products never quite get past the innovator group while others may simultaneously reach the earlier adopter groups and the majority segment. Furthermore, many products, after many decades of being in the market, still show no sign of reaching the laggards. As a matter of fact, numerous products survive longer and more happily than their adopters. Camel, the first nationally distributed cigarette brand, is still one of the top sellers after several decades.

Exhibit 4.2 also provides information on a special case of adoption—the fad product. When compared with the regular adoption curve, the fad adoption curve indicates that a fad achieves a greater market penetration within a shorter time period. However, the very nature of a fad product also dictates saturation and abandonment in much the same abrupt fashion as the way the product was initially accepted in the market. As shown in the case of video games, the product peaked rapidly and saturated the market within weeks of introduction. In 1983, the craze suddenly stopped and the market for video games collapsed.

Regardless of whether a product is a staple item or a fashion product, the size (number of adopters) will greatly vary from one adopter category to another. The disproportionate distribution of adopters among the five adopter categories is caused by the interactive effect as well as the lack of it. The minimal interaction occurring early in the introductory stage results in only a few consumers being innovators. With the passage of time and an increase in the number of individuals who are aware of the product's existence, there will inevitably be more and more interaction, facilitating the process of influence and imitation. This kind of social influence creates a snowball effect and should lead to a large number of purchasers entering the rapid-growth stage of the product. If there is a lack of the interactive effect, the probability of adopting the product should be equal for all five groups, resulting in the same proportion of adopters for each stage.

ADOPTER CATEGORIES

While innovators are important and have received a great deal of attention among researchers, the other four adopter categories also deserve the same kind of interest. After all, marketers must depend on subsequent adopters for revenues and profits sooner or later, given the fact that these adopters are the mass market.

Innovators are venturesome consumers with above average status. This group has some opinion leadership, even though most of the opinion leadership takes place in the next adopter category. While innovativeness and opinion leadership are positively related, innovators and opinion leaders are technically not the same. It is thus possible to be an innovator without being an opinion leader, and vice versa.

Innovators are low-risk perceivers who primarily depend on impersonal sources of information when making purchase decisions. They are socially mobile, financially privileged, cosmopolitan, and more likely to travel. These characteristics are logical because innovators must be aware of world events and new ideas, and they must also have adequate funds to pay for the initial high prices of many new products.

It should be pointed out that innovators are less likely to try new convenience items if such items merely represent minor changes. Moreover, they are less interested in price per se. These two determinants mean that innovators are more interested in product benefits than prices. Therefore, a low price appeal is generally ineffective with innovators since it is not a substitute for product advantages. Prices therefore should be kept initially high in order to generate more profit.

Just because innovators are the earliest buyers, it should not be presumed that they are hasty purchasers. Usually innovators will purchase a new item only after they are convinced of the product's value. The purchase is initiated after adequate information is gathered and careful thinking done. Thus, innovators are not necessarily impulsive purchasers, and they tend to be receptive to information provided by advertisers.

Early adopters are highly respected. They are able to command respect from others because of their high social status. It is not uncommon for early adopters to be organizational leaders or to come from the professional and managerial ranks. Neither should it be surprising that this group has the greatest opinion leadership of all the adopter categories. Early adopters' prestige and strategic social location make it a given for them to influence others.

Early adopters have high income with slightly above-average education levels. They hold more group memberships and are well integrated into their social system. In contrast, there is a question of whether innovators are in the middle or at the edge of the social system. It is conceivable that innovators are "mavericks" who adopt new products because they are not too concerned with traditional ideas and group norms.

While innovators are influenced mainly by impersonal information sources, early adopters are more broadly information based. Much like innovators, early adopters pay attention to information provided by mass media. In addition, early adopters also have the benefit of being able to observe and to consult with innovators. In this regard, word-of-mouth and mass media are equally important in their decision making.

The *early majority* group is deliberate. The members of this group consider a new product only after it has gained their peers' acceptance. They possess slightly above-average education and status. Some opinion leadership also occurs within this group. While early majority consumers have some exposure to mass media, they depend more on informal or personal sources of information in their attempt to minimize the chance of making an incorrect purchasing decision.

The *late majority* group is known for being skeptical. Consumers from the late majority category usually adopt a new product only after either being strongly pressured by their peers or being vividly shown the advantage of the innovation over other products. The first condition means that late majority consumers may stand a high chance of being ridiculed by their peers and thus a reference group appeal in advertising can be effective in forcing them to accept the new product. The second condition, on the other hand, implies that, for the late majority to adopt the product, there must be no question in their minds that the innovation is superior to existing products. To convince these purchasers of the product's value, comparative advertising should be used. It should also be noted that this group is somewhat below average in terms of status and income. Some opinion leadership still exists, but in most cases the late majority is influenced primarily by word-of-mouth in making purchases.

Laggards are considered to be traditional. They tend to be older and have the lowest status and income and very little opinion leadership. Opinion leadership does exist in every social class and adopter category, but its proportion varies. Laggards normally depend on personal sources such as neighbors and friends for information. This group, while being late in the adoption of the product, is still important to the marketer since it provides sales volume, especially when innovators may be moving on to other products. Furthermore, laggards are valuable because they tend to be brand loyal—something which innovators are not.

There is often a strong pro-innovation bias which is developed and encouraged by advertisers and sometimes implies that nonadoption is an individual or social failure.[1] But many innovations such as cigarettes and illegal drugs are not always socially beneficial. Also any innovation, even when generally useful, is not necessarily desirable for all consumers. A substantial portion of a population may reject the product either because of product inferiority or product incompatibility with consumer lifestyles. For consumers who rejected such unsuccessful products as four-channel high fidelity sound equipment and the videodisc, these nonadopters apparently made a better decision than the adopters of these products. Adopters of Rely tampons, to their dismay, found that tampons in general and Rely in particular, might be associated with toxic shock syndrome. Should nonadopters in such cases be classified as "true" innovators by the virtue of their superior decision (i.e., recognition and rejection of new but undesirable products)? The possible redefinition of what constitutes an innovator based on this analysis is intriguing and should be further investigated.

IMPORTANCE OF INNOVATORS

Theoretically, innovators are the most important of the five adopter groups for a number of reasons. First, for a product to ever get into the growth stage, the product must gain innovators' acceptance. Without innovators' support, retailers will not carry or continue to carry the new product. Second, innovators help expand the market by influencing other potential purchasers. Providing legitimation, innovators may directly encourage others to adopt the product by explaining the product's benefits to others. Innovators' influence can also be indirect in the sense that communication is provided to others through the social display of product use. The indirect influence can be broadened if the observers turn out to be opinion leaders who will relay the information to others. Finally, innovators tend to be heavy users of the product. In comparison with late adopters, innovators use the accepted product more often or in a larger quantity because they either are more convinced of the value of the product or know how to derive more benefits out of it.

CONSUMER CHARACTERISTICS ASSOCIATED WITH INNOVATIVENESS

Given the importance of innovators, marketers should identify those characteristics which influence innovativeness so that the characteristics can be used to effectively communicate with innovators and thus influence innovativeness. Some researchers approach this problem by investigating consumer characteristics; others, by examining product characteristics.

In terms of consumer characteristics associated with innovativeness, innovators tend to be above average in education, income, and occupational status. Innovators are also relatively young, and young people tend to be less conservative and more willing to accept the risks associated with a new product or idea. Innovators are socially active and physically and socially mobile, and such experiences may make them aware of new products and ideas and prepare the way for innovative purchases. Not surprisingly, innovators are cosmopolitan, and this is consistent with their mobile tendency.

In terms of personality, innovators are venturesome, indicating a willingness to take risks. Innovators tend not to be dogmatic and will thus approach new products with considerable openness and minimal anxiety. Furthermore, they are inner-directed, relying more on their inner values in making decisions about new products and less on others for guidance.

With regard to media habits, innovators tend to have more exposure to selective media (relevant to the product of interest) but not to mass media in general. Thus, TV viewership is not related to innovativeness because this medium is intended for large numbers of people with varying interests. The positive correlation between print readership and innovativeness, on the other hand, means that innovators pay more attention to special-interest media such as magazines that are highly subject-selective.

Although innovators have identifiable characteristics, ranging from demographics to media habits, that are significantly different from those of later buyers, the relationship between innovativeness and these characteristics varies greatly from product to product. In this regard, many of the generalizations that are stated are more applicable to durable products than to low-cost, grocery products. Additionally, it is incorrect to assume that these generalizations will hold true for all durable products. For example, although innovators of several durable goods tend to be relatively young and to have higher status occupations with higher incomes and education, early buyers of the rotary-engine Mazda automobile provided little verification for these characteristics.

Is it possible to identify a generalized innovator who accepts every new product before others consistently? Are innovators born and thus innovation-prone? Innovators are not born, and their characteristics are product specific. A few studies which have been done show that overlap of product innovativeness is not great and that it tends to occur only for related products. Innovators of CD (compact disc) players are likely to be interested in DAT (digital audio tape) players because such products are highly related. This does not mean, however, that they must also be interested in other electronic products or services such as ABC's scrambled broadcasts after 2 A.M. which were tried but quickly folded.

Appliances, clothing, and food innovators, likewise, have been shown to be statistically related—but not very strongly. This low level of correlation indicates that innovativeness is not a general trait. Therefore, characteristics of innovators for each product category must be determined individually.

THEORY AND PRACTICE

Marketing scholars, citing the high rate of new product failure, repeatedly admonish practitioners for not applying or incorporating the adoption process into their marketing plans where new product introductions are involved. As far as some marketing theorists are concerned, a new product can only be successful if and when innovators, not other adopter groups, are appealed to effectively. It thus becomes necessary to identify innovators and to promote the new product to them accordingly. It is unfortunate that many marketing instructors who try to teach students about the marketing application of diffusion theory find it very difficult to provide examples of how to use the theory once an explanation of it has been provided. This difficulty is thought to develop because the diffusion of innovations theory does not fit well with the marketing mix due to a lack of distribution, pricing, and promotion strategies that are oriented toward the innovator. A further problem is not so much how to identify innovators but rather why innovators should be singled out in the first place. What are the marketing purposes that innovators are supposed to serve, and if the diffusion process is so useful, why has it been ignored for so long by marketing managers?[2]

To be useful, a theory that is relevant to marketing must be tied to a marketing strategy through the use of an appropriate marketing mix. Unfortunately, this is not the case with diffusion theory. While the theory suffers from various shortcomings, its most serious problem is its lack of marketing applicability. When product, distribution, promotion, and pricing strategies are offered, they are vaguely and weakly stated; more often than not, they are conspicuous by their absence.

A Product Problem

The diffusion process contributes very little to marketing mix strategies as far as a product policy is concerned. It does not make any recommendations with regard to product quality, product variations for market segmentation, and product features for product differentiation. In regard to product deletion, the diffusion theory fails to specify how to identify product maturity and when a company should transfer resources to other products to maintain profit levels.

A product may have more than one life cycle. The situation can become much more complicated when obsolete products are suddenly "in" again, while their counterparts are on the way out. Some time ago consumers gave up coal as a viable source of energy, and nuclear energy, on the other hand, became the energy hope for the future. Within just a few short years, the situation has been completely reversed. The question we need to ask now is: Are users of coal laggards or innovators? Apparently, this is only one of many questions that remain unanswered within the context of current diffusion theory.

Any attempt to develop a product policy based on diffusion theory also presents difficulties because the theory makes no distinction among product class, form, and brand. It is not known whether the diffusion process is applicable for all three product levels or just for any one of the levels. At the product class level, it is not clear whether innovation diffusion theory should be applied to infrequently purchased durable goods or to products rapidly consumed and used repeatedly. As stated earlier, it is difficult to say whether a significantly modified product should be considered a continuous extension of an existing diffusion or the start of a new diffusion altogether. A Toro compact snowblower designed for areas of light snowfall, for example, is a modification of its heavy-duty, bulky counterpart. How should adopters of the smaller version be classified?

There is no question that the compact disc (CD), when first introduced, was a brand new product with its own diffusion curve. But in the case of the Ford Mustang (which has been modified over the years) or in the case of "new" Coke, it is difficult to say with certainty whether they are indeed new products.

The same problem exists at the product form level. Users of one product form, say, a tape deck, are unlikely to have a need for the other two forms of tape decks. Should they be classified automatically as nonadopters of the other two product forms? Milk consumption has been declining significantly for many years, and the milk industry is now trying to retard any further erosion by introducing new flavors. For a person trying a new milk flavor (e.g., orange flavor or cherry flavor), is this consumer an innovator given the fact that milk itself has been in existence for so long?

Finally, at the product brand level, should innovators for each brand be identified separately? Does each brand have its own diffusion independent of the product form? When brands are significantly different, it may be justified to classify them in this way. But brands usually compete strongly and try to take market share from each other, implying that their customers are somehow alike. Cigarette firms have flooded the market with new brands in the low-tar category. Does the diffusion process apply only to the low-tar product form, or should it be applicable to each brand (i.e., each brand having its own diffusion independent of the product form)? The lack of distinction and definition makes the situation very confusing: early buyers of a new brand are innovators for that brand, and yet they may be nothing more than late adopters on an industry-wide basis.

A Distribution Problem

Some authorities claim that a distribution system should be designed with innovators in mind. But is it practical for the marketer to do so? To design a distribution system for innovators who are small in number and low in brand loyalty is difficult to justify, especially when another distribution channel may have to be later developed for the mass market. The price paid for such a recommendation would be prohibitively high and in all likelihood would create ill will among middlemen of competing systems. Perhaps the diffusion process could become more meaningful, but only when innovations are somehow classified so that each product category could be tied to certain types of wholesale and retail institutions. The theory in its present form does not make any useful contribution in determining the length and width of a distribution channel.

A Pricing Problem

The diffusion theory suggests that price should be kept high in the initial stage of an innovation since innovators are financially privileged and are not interested in a low price per se. This kind of reasoning does not take into account the fact that to break into a market, many firms use a penetration (low-price) pricing strategy.

There is no denying, however, that many firms do indeed use a high-price or skimming pricing strategy. But this strategy is hardly inspired by the diffusion theory. Instead, it is usually influenced by the "learning curve" hypothesis which states that price must be kept high until the manufacturing process and workers can become skilled at producing products more efficiently at a lower cost. A high price initially is also caused by another competing theory—product life cycle (PLC). According to the PLC concept, the price should be set high in the introductory stage because of the small volume of sales, inefficient production and marketing, frequent product modifications, few competitors, and a desire to recover research and development costs as soon as possible in an uncertain market. Therefore, as a competing theory the product life cycle concept may be more appropriate and can make valuable pricing recommendations just as much as the diffusion theory.

A Promotion Problem

The very preliminary promotional problem that may exist with in-novators is that, since innovativeness cannot be expected across product categories unless they are closely related, a marketer may have to identify innovators for each product individually. The problem, however, is that innovators cannot be conclusively identified until after they have pur-chased the product in question. By the time these innovators are known, the need to appeal to them no longer exists. By that time, the marketer should be concentrating on other potential adopters. In these circum-stances, it appears that the marketer may often be one step behind in effecting the appropriate marketing strategy.

Even if it could be assumed that innovators can be identified suffi-ciently early for marketers to influence them in some way, the costs involved would be prohibitive. First, if a unique advertising appeal is developed just for innovators, such a campaign may discourage other potential buyers. Innovators, by their very nature, are cosmopolitan, and a cosmopolitan approach may have to be used in order to appeal to them. But by making an innovation appear very cosmopolitan, it may subsequently alienate other adopter groups if they do not share this same trait. On the other hand, it is also difficult to understand how it could be practical for marketers to develop one advertising appeal for innovators and another appeal for late adopters. Constant changes in product positioning would seem to contradict a sound marketing prac-tice. When the same product is positioned differently for different con-sumer groups, consumers can easily become confused by the various appeals. Another consideration is the high costs associated with devel-oping different appeals for each adopter group.

Secondly, marketers may still not have identified the means to reach innovators with minimum waste. Most advertising media (including radio and magazines) are far from being selective, and an inevitable consequence of this is that a great deal of promotion waste follows because too many non-innovators are being reached at the same time. Thus, the diffusion process has very little value in the sense that ad-vertisers cannot efficiently communicate with those purposefully iden-tified by the process.

It is an accepted fact that most products have a difficult time surviving in the market without the support of mass market purchases. As a result, it may be a mistake to attempt to reach innovators at the very onset of the diffusion process. Both positive and negative innovators exist, and negative innovators (i.e., those who dislike the adopted product) can induce negative diffusion upon the adoption process. On the occasion when a marketer is able to reach innovators successfully and then is turned down by negative innovators, this rejection experience can se-

verely affect the mass market. On the other hand, success is not necessarily guaranteed by the acceptance of a product by innovators,
especially when the innovators are conceptually different from non-
innovators. The Edsel automobile is a prime example of a product that
was accepted by innovators but rejected by the mass market.

Marketers' failure to apply the diffusion process theory in practice can
hardly be used as the reason for such poor performance in the marketplace. For the present, there is little evidence that marketers are taking
the diffusion process seriously, and it is difficult to fault them for not
doing so. Marketers have concentrated their efforts on the mainstream
of the market (i.e., the early and late majority mass markets) without
much attention to the innovator. This attitude reflecting the unimport-
ance of the innovator is likely to continue unless changes are made
concerning the significance of the innovator in the diffusion process. In
all likelihood, this will mean a fundamental review and a very practical
look at the true role of the innovator in the diffusion process. Not until
this is done can the marketing practitioner confidently direct his marketing effort at the innovator. An early serious marketing effort directed
to the innovator could result in a ripple effect that would augment later
marketing efforts and create a synergistic effect within the product adoption process as it moves through the later diffusion stages.

PRODUCT CHARACTERISTICS ASSOCIATED WITH PRODUCT ADOPTION

The past focus of the diffusion theory has been on consumer characteristics, a side of the consumer that is uncontrollable by marketers.
Demographic, social, and psychological variables may exert a great deal
of influence on consumer choice, but marketing managers are basically
powerless to affect such variables. Too little attention, on the other hand,
has been devoted to an analysis of product characteristics. This is unfortunate, because these characteristics are concrete, identifiable, and
controllable.

In studies of how product characteristics affect the rate of diffusion,
five product variables have been identified and have gained widespread
acceptance: relative advantage, compatibility, observability, trialability,
and complexity. While the use of these five characteristics has been
traditional, the examination is not complete without taking two other
important variables—perceived risk and price—into account. It must be
stressed that these seven characteristics are not necessarily objective
since all are based on consumer perception. A consumer may view a
new product as an advantage even though the benefit is merely imaginary. Conversely, that product may be quite simple yet it may be

perceived as complex. It is this kind of perception that will be discussed next.

Relative Advantage

Relative advantage is the perceived desirability or the benefit derived from a new product relative to those benefits offered by other existing products. For the new product to gain rapid acceptance, the product must be seen as being more attractive than other alternatives. The product's attributes that are being used for differentiation purposes must also be perceived as both good and significant.

The relationship between perceived advantage and innovativeness is positive: the greater the perceived advantage, the more likely it is that the product will be adopted. For example, the addition of a Dolby noise reduction system to tape recorders was perceived as a major advantage. Not only did tape recorder sales increase dramatically, but so did the sales of chromium dioxide tapes used with tape recorders equipped with the Dolby system. The same can be said about the development of high fidelity equipment. The stereo (two-channel) system with its capability for sound separation is perceived as being much better than the original monophonic system. In contrast, the quadraphonic (four-channel) system, promoted with much excitement, did not gain widespread acceptance because it was not perceived as a significant improvement over the stereo system. After all, a listener only has two ears, and may not perceive that four speakers offer any significant advantage over two speakers.

Facsimile machines, due to their relative advantage, are beginning to threaten the existence of two products: overnight mailing and telex services. A facsimile message is faster and less expensive than overnight delivery service. It also has the advantage over telex that a facsimile message provides a photocopy of the original document while telex or electronic mail cannot offer pictures or signatures. Since the introduction of facsimile machines, the U.S. telex business dropped from 397 million minutes in 1984 to less than 200 million minutes in 1987.

A dedicated word processor is a computer that has a detached keyboard and a built-in video screen and is capable of operating with word processing software. As a special kind of computer, it is a product created for all the wrong reasons. First, it has no significant advantage over a personal computer. A dedicated word processor lacks power and versatility since it can perform only one function—word processing. No other operational tasks, business or recreational, are possible on such a unit. Yet the dedicated word processor is just as expensive as a personal computer while not being any easier to use. With all these built-in limitations, it is difficult to understand why anyone would want to own a dedicated word processor.

Compatibility

A new product should be compatible with the experiences, values, lifestyles, religious beliefs, and attitudes of consumers in the target market as well as with other products in their possession. When inconsistency occurs, the new product necessitates changes in thinking and attitude. Subsequently, the diffusion process is slowed down. The Amish, for example, have long resisted such products as automobiles, vaccines, electricity, and so forth, since these products are not consistent with the self-sufficiency principle by which the Amish live.

For every winner, there are many losers, and the midi is an example of a product that was not a winner. In 1970, the garment industry, with support from designers, manufacturers, and retailers, tried to make existing wardrobes obsolete by introducing the midi-skirts, which fall below the knee, with ankle-length skirts as the most heavily promoted. This abrupt change from the mini style to midis in order to stimulate sales ran into a great deal of consumer opposition. As a result, more than 60 expensive dressmakers were forced out of business, while retailers were also badly harmed because of unsold inventory. This spectacular failure was caused by several factors: (1) the midi was psychologically restrictive at the time when women demanded more freedom, (2) ankle-length midis were unflattering, impractical, and prone to accidents, (3) recession and inflation left consumers with little discretionary income to replace now obsolete existing wardrobes, and (4) the weather at the time was too warm. Had the hemline been gradually lengthened, a different kind of reaction may have resulted. The midi example points out the fact that a product can fail because it is not quite compatible with the public mood at the time.

Compaq's strategy in marketing its Compaq Portable computer was so successful that the product was responsible for most of the company's sales in its first year. The company's idea of compatibility and portability was revolutionary at the time. By making its machine IBM-compatible, Compaq offered its customers the assurance of having a computer that was compatible with the industry standard.

After having an unsuccessful experience with its desk-top personal computers, Digital Equipment Corp. (DEC) decided to make its personal computers more compatible with those of its competitors. As a first move, DEC agreed to become compatible with the Macintosh system. In quick succession, it also embraced the IBM OS/2 and UNIX standards. DEC's approach was a wise move, given the fact that computer users were unhappy with computers of different designs which were unable to communicate with each other. The problem of incompatibility eventually forced a dozen computer makers, which accounted for more than 80 percent of the computer and communications sales, to adopt a set of uniform standards (Open Systems Interconnect Standard) in 1988.

Observability or Communicability

The quality of observability is concerned with whether the use of a new product is publicly visible or not. A product will have a better chance of success if it is socially or publicly consumed rather than being privately used. The public use and consumption of a product helps increase visibility and identification. If the product is visible in social situations and if its features can easily be communicated among consumers, the chance that it will be successful will be increased accordingly. One reason why the quadraphonic high fidelity system did not gain wide acceptance was because it was not highly visible. The picturephone is another product which has encountered a similar problem and fate.

Trialability or Divisibility

Consumers are more likely to try a new product if they do not have to commit themselves to a long period of time or a substantial sum of money. If a product can be subdivided so that it can be tried in small quantities, consumers are more likely to try it. That is, the more that a product can be divided or tried, the more likely it will gain acceptance. G. D. Searle found from its research that consumers initially tried smaller sizes of its Equal sugar substitute before moving up to 100 or 200 packets for convenience and better value.

When a consumer is forced to initially buy in large quantities, the adverse consequence of making a mistake is simply too great for most consumers. Such a high risk will then slow down the acceptance of the innovation. In the case of the picturephone, it is not highly visible, in addition to not being divisible. Picturephone innovators also had to pay a substantial sum for installation as well as a $100 monthly service fee. With such high costs, it is not surprising that this product had to be withdrawn from the various trial cities.

The marketing implication from this product's experience is that marketers should use samples to gain product trial and adoption. This strategy is often employed by perfume, cigarette, and candy bar manufacturers. In the case that a product cannot be divided or that a sample cannot be provided, marketers can solve the problem by employing a demonstration strategy. A free sample of an automobile, for example, is impractical, but a test drive is of benefit. In this same vein,

Apple used to offer potential buyers a chance to take its Macintosh computer home for a "24-hour test drive."

Complexity

Complexity involves the relative difficulty (or ease) of understanding how a product operates. When the product is highly complex and difficult to understand and use, product acceptance is delayed. Individuals usually seek consistency and understanding and will hesitate adopting products which they do not understand. One reason why the Mazda was not very successful when it was first introduced in the United States was because potential buyers did not understand the operation of a rotary engine.

Coldsnap was a make-at-home ice cream product. This boxed mix consisting of a powder and gelatinous substance could be blended with milk. Once frozen, it became an ice-cream-like dessert. The problem with this product was that there was no good reason why consumers would want to make a product that they could easily and conveniently buy at the supermarket. In the minds of consumers, it furthermore made no sense to turn something easy into something difficult. The result was that Coldsnap was quickly withdrawn from the test market when these problems became evident.

Perceived Risk

In addition to its relative advantage attributes, a product may also have inherent disadvantages as perceived by consumers. Such risks may include physical, functional, social, psychological, and financial risks. There are always some risks which are associated with a new product. The risks may range from serious physical harm from the product to annoyance when the product fails to operate correctly. It is thus logical to assume a negative relationship between perceived risk and innovativeness. Innovators are risk takers who either do not visualize risk in using a new product or simply are not concerned about risk. For example, new drugs are usually accompanied by unknown side effects. But innovators do not see any harm in trying these drugs, or they may believe that other conventional drugs are just as risky.

Electronic home banking, first introduced in 1980, is another product which has failed to gain consumer acceptance. This service allows users to connect their personal computers to their bank's mainframe computer in order to perform such tasks as money transfers, bill payments, and the examination of balances in checking accounts and credit card accounts. Home banking appears to have more perceived drawbacks than perceived benefits. One major problem seems to be the perceived risks connected with the service. Users fear errors and dislike the immediate debit and elimination of the float. Additionally, the advantages provided by electronic home banking can be, for the most part, provided through conventional banking methods. Moreover, the cost of home banking is approximately $10 a month, and, although offered at a loss by the bank, is too high for most consumers.

Price

Price and innovativeness are negatively related, and high price is a deterrent to adoption. When products are new, prices usually need to be high because of small volume and the lack of economies of scale. But as demonstrated by the life cycles of many products, mass production makes it possible for prices to decline. The decline in prices will in turn stimulate sales. The initial price of the Sony Betamax video recorder, for example, was above $2,000 before falling to well below $1,000. Likewise, sales of calculators and C B radios increased rapidly when prices were decreased. It can now be anticipated that personal computers will gain rapid acceptance since prices for various sytems have substantially declined.

Low price has the tendency of speeding up the trial phase and adoption process since the negative consequences of making a wrong decision are minimized. Price is one reason why credit card companies, despite their large losses due to fraud, have continued to offer conventional credit cards which cost seven cents a card to manufacture. In contrast, the so-called smart cards which contain an embedded computer chip cost an estimated $5 a card. Furthermore, to accommodate the new cards, some four million terminals in use in the United States would have to be replaced. The cost of switching to the new, superior technology would cost MasterCard and VISA half a billion dollars each.

A good innovation should score relatively high with regard to the first four product variables, whereas the innovation should score low on the last three attributes. It should be noted that these degrees are determined by consumer perception, which may not necessarily be related to reality or the qualities actually inherent in the new product. In any case, the first four product attributes contribute positively to product adoption, while the last three are negatively related to product acceptance.

The product characteristics mentioned have been found to be better predictors of purchase outcome than respondent personal characteristics. For example, adopters of solar energy systems rated such systems significantly higher than nonusers on relative advantage and compatibility and lower on complexity.[3] These findings are good news for marketers since product characteristics and not consumer variables are what marketers can control. The actual marketing applications given below explain how consumer resistance can be turned into acceptance by making adjustments in product characteristics.

Due to the importance of the product attributes mentioned above, researchers should experiment more with these variables to determine their relative contribution and relationship with the rate of diffusion. For marketers, advantages would be gained by not placing so much emphasis on the significance of the innovator and his qualifications (i.e., demographic and personality characteristics). Instead, marketers should pay more attention to product aspects that do indeed affect the product adoption rate. After all, demographic and personality characteristics are very elusive and often vary across adopter groups. In contrast, the seven product characteristics remain constant across adopter categories, and a product that satisfies these characteristics in the prescribed manner will satisfy all consumers in the target market simultaneously, regardless of whether they are innovators or not.

SOME EXAMPLES OF THE MARKETING UTILIZATION OF PRODUCT CHARACTERISTICS

In the view of knowledgeable camera users, there has never been any doubt that 35-mm cameras have significant advantages over pocket 110 cameras in terms of quality, flexibility, and prestige. The acceptance of the 35-mm camera took a long time, however, because of problems related to certain product characteristics, mainly complexity and price. "The development of low-cost integrated circuits, cheap but durable plastics, and automated manufacturing techniques" makes it possible to now mass produce high-quality but low-priced cameras. Regarding complexity, Canon spent $15 million using John Newcombe, Ben Crenshaw, and other athletes to convince potential buyers that, with its new single-lens reflex camera, all they have to do is to "aim and shoot." As a result of this effort, Canon's U.S. sales were 500 percent above the sales level of 1974. Since then, the popularity of 35-mm cameras has become so great that Kodak, after many years of resistance, has decided to offer this product form in the late 1980s.

It is evident that soft contact lenses provide consumers with more freedom and, perhaps, a better appearance than conventional eyeglasses. Yet, out of some 70 million potential buyers, less than 10 percent wear soft contact lens. Consumers are deterred from adoption because of three important product characteristics: (1) price, (2) perceived risk (fear of putting something in their eyes), and (3) communicability—"how soft is soft?" Consumers can easily see that price has already declined and that stores urge consumers to "try" them before buying in an effort to increase trialability. With regard to perceived risk and communicability, American Optical used advertisements to demonstate how easily its soft lens bends when placed between the petals of a rose.

It is just a matter of time—very likely in the not too distant future—that conventional vinyl records will be completely replaced by compact discs (CDs). This development is very likely inevitable because the CD is far superior to the vinyl record in a number of ways. As a laser-based, computerized technology, the CD offers superior quality in sound reproduction. In addition to the ability to store more minutes of music, the CD presents no problems with scratches, smudges, and heat warping. CD manufacturers have also made it easier for consumers to adopt the product. They have agreed on a five-inch standard for discs while making certain that CD players can be used with existing sound equipment and components. Although the prices for CDs and CD players were initially high, the prices have dropped significantly. Not surprisingly, in just a few short years, the sales of CDs soared from 17 million in 1983 to 103 million in 1984, 389 million in 1985, and 930 million 1986.

CONCLUSION

Despite optimistic forecasts, many products fail. It is difficult to predict the success of a new product due to a number of reasons. First, for a truly new product, there are no precedents which can be used as guidelines for success. Moreover, the market, culture, and consumers are dynamic and unpredictable and complicate the situation. A change in any of the three can significantly alter the predicted outcome.

As evidenced by the high number of product failures, consumers are becoming more unpredictable and more difficult to satisfy. Marketers' failure to apply the diffusion process theory in practice should not be used as the reason for such poor performance in the marketplace. Generally speaking, it appears that diffusion theory as currently understood offers very little practical application. Very few meaningful recommendations are made and, when they are offered, such recommendations are vague as well as impractical.

The innovator does have a key role in the diffusion process and perhaps the time has come to take another look at and provide a redefinition of the innovator's role in the diffusion process. A new view would go some distance in re-establishing the credibility of the diffusion process and its place in the development of marketing strategy. Perhaps proponents of this theory must initially understand that the real innovators are actually marketers who must be convinced of the idea before they adopt and apply it in practice.

An understanding of the diffusion process of innovations is critical if a new product is to have a good chance of surviving and succeeding in the marketplace. The success of a new product depends on consumer characteristics as well as product characteristics. Innovativeness for durables, for example, is related to certain consumer characteristics such as demographics, opinion leadership, and a limited number of personality variables. The direction of that association, however, often varies across product categories, meaning that innovators for each product may have to be determined and appealed to separately.

A shift in research priority and approach is also recommended. On one front, future studies should focus on *product characteristics* because these characteristics significantly affect the adoption rate and are controllable. Moreover, this aspect has received relatively sparse attention. In contrast, consumer characteristics as related to the diffusion process of innovations have been exhaustively studied, but these variables are largely beyond the marketer's control.

Product characteristics are conceivably even more important than consumer variables in exerting influence over the rates of diffusion. Innovativeness tends to vary positively with perceived advantage, compatibility, observability, and divisibility. This very same variable is, however, negatively related to complexity, perceived risk, and price. It may be possible that there is a great deal that the marketer can do by mixing and modifying these product characteristics in such a way as to enhance and encourage adoption.

While it is generally accepted that innovativeness is positively related to relative advantage, compatibility, observability, and trialability and negatively related to complexity, perceived risk, and price, very few studies go beyond the basic discussion of the relationships to estimate the relative importance of each characteristic. Such rankings of importance are critical if the marketer is to minimize the risk of stressing the wrong product characteristic in his promotional campaign.

NOTES

1. Everett M. Rogers, "New Product Adoption and Diffusion," in *Selected Aspects of Consumer Behavior: A Summary from the Different Disciplines, RANN Program* (Washington, D.C.: National Science Foundation, 1976), pp. 223–38.

2. For further discussion, see Sak Onkvisit and John J. Shaw, "The Diffusion of Innovations Theory: Some Research Questions," *Akron Business and Economic Review*, forthcoming; Sak Onkvisit and John J. Shaw, "The Diffusion of Innovations Theory: Some Theoretical Questions," *Proceedings*, Southern Marketing Association Conference, 1987, pp. 198–201; and Sak Onkvisit and John J. Shaw, "Present and Future Implications for the Diffusion of Innovations Theory within the Marketplace," *Proceedings*, Northeast Business and Economics Association Conference, 1986, pp. 113–14.

3. Duncan G. LaBay and Thomas C. Kinnear, "Exploring the Consumer Decision Process in the Adoption of Solar Energy Systems," *Journal of Consumer Research* 8 (December 1981): 271–78.

PART III

PRODUCT LIFE CYCLE MANAGEMENT

5

Product Life Cycle: The Marketing Mix

WHAT GOES UP MUST COME DOWN

Salt was so valuable at one time that it was used as money (i.e., a medium of exchange). Its fortune (as well as its value) has, however, come down with time. As evidenced by the figures showing table salt usage in the United States, the annual consumption has been dropping by about 2 percent annually, and it appears that this trend will continue. As a matter of fact, it is likely that the consumption of salt will decline even more rapidly in the future because consumers are becoming increasingly concerned about the effect of salt on health.

The taste for salt is not innate but acquired. American consumers' perception of salt has taken a turn for the worse. Salt is now perceived as being inherently bad due to its link to heart and health problems. As a result, almost three-quarters of adults want to reduce their salt intake.[1] To capitalize on this trend, R. C. Cola used the "salt assault" advertising campaign for its Salt-free Diet Rite soft drink. Armour Food, likewise, offered a new line of lower-salt meat (bacon, ham, sausage, lunch meats, and hot dogs) and cheese products. Such products can now come out of the closet since they no longer have to be sold as dietetic items and confined to that aisle.

The demand for paper used to be very high while supplies tended to be on the scarce side. Despite this strong demand, the paper market has never really recovered from the 1974–75 recession. Furthermore, though paper is a convenient medium for message recording, other means, in recent years, have become popular for message recording. Now no longer a growth industry, paper has become just another mature product facing a bleak future due to the possibility that we may become a paperless society. Optical discs, personal computers, video systems, and telecommunications systems are all electronic media which are being adapted for such tasks as electronic catalogs, newspapers, and journals. Newspaper print usage of paper alone will be reduced by 800,000 metric tons or 15 percent of present annual consumption by the year 1995.

PRODUCT LIFE CYCLE: A STRATEGIC CONCEPT

A product is much like a tree growing in a new forest. Some will die early while others will grow to maturity. Those which survive, however, will not do equally well. The dominant trees are likely to be the attractive ones: they command attention and will be noticed by people walking in the forest. Just like the attractive tree, a successful product is often a unique one. But as young saplings turn into mature trees (and products get older), the older trees face more problems—weather damage, disease, or being cut down for lumber (or in the case of products, new technological breakthroughs). Some trees are successful in fending off problems—at least for a while—by resisting disease or being overlooked by the woodsman. But sooner or later, old age does catch up, and the health of the tree will deteriorate. A decline stage usually follows with trees and products becoming old, passing on, and being replaced by others.

The purpose of the above analogy is to demonstrate the changes and problems faced by trees and products. Just like trees, products go through stages or cycles. Furthermore, some products will survive just as long as some of their natural counterparts, implying that the life of a product can almost be indefinitely extended, if appropriately supported. Thus, it is critical to identify and understand the stages that a product passes through as it survives. The competitive characteristics will vary from stage to stage—some for the better; others for the worse—necessitating some timely adjustments in the marketing strategies. A failure to understand these changes and to adjust the marketing mix may result in a premature death for a product. The two marketing examples of salt and paper cited earlier should serve to emphasize the significance of making a division among these distinct stages. That is what an analysis of the product life cycle is supposed to entail.

Product life cycle (PLC), a popular concept in marketing, identifies four discrete stages of a product: introduction, growth, maturation, and decline. A few authors go beyond these usual stages, but their finer, more detailed classifications do not seem to contribute any significant distinctions beyond the usual four basic stages mentioned above. The product life cycle curve depicting the four stages and its corresponding profit curve is shown in Exhibit 5.1. Exhibit 5.2 describes the major changes occurring to product characteristics.[2] Each product stage is explained below in more detail.

INTRODUCTION STAGE

The first stage of product life cycle is the "introduction" of a new product that suggests that a new way has been determined to satisfy either a new or existing need. It is also known as the "pioneering" stage because there are usually only one or a few pioneering firms which are willing to take the chance in bringing a new product to the market. The number of competitors is at a minimum as businessmen deliberately avoid being pioneers, especially when it is more likely that a new product will fail rather than succeed. In many cases, most of the competition will not come so much from direct competition (i.e., other brands) but rather from indirect competitors (i.e., other product classes and/or forms) since they are all trying to compete for the consumer's limited income.

When first introduced, the videodisc player competed mainly with video cassette recorders (VCRs) and 16-mm (conventional) movie cameras. In its turn, Polavision (instant movie) came along to challenge the VCR briefly before bowing out of the picture because consumers failed

Exhibit 5.1
Product Life Cycle and Profit Curves

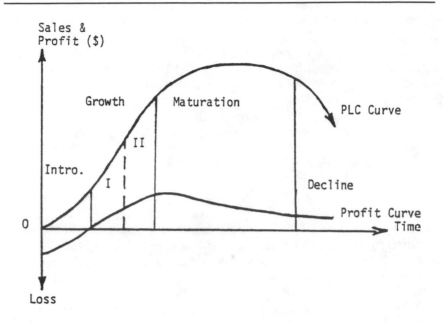

to perceive how the instant movie could be superior to the VCR which can record and erase, in addition to having a playback feature.

In many situations, new products may find industrial application first (e.g., video cassette recorder), and later application and purchase within the consumer market. As new products are introduced to market, sales usually rise rather slowly with the high income consumer target market because many new products (especially high unit-value ones) can only be afforded by financially privileged persons, unless the products are specifically aimed at lower-income groups. Compact disc players were marketed initially with the top of the pyramid buyers in mind. These buyers were those males between 25 and 45 years old who were upwardly mobile with discretionary income. They were in the managerial rank and had a great deal of interest in music.

It is not unusual for a new product to have functional problems, because corrective refinements have not been completely worked out within the product. When first introduced, the automatic garage door opener was frequently activated by mistake by other drivers or when a pilot talked to a controller. Likewise, cordless phones, as a radio, initially had problems of interference, security, and eavesdropping. Metallic

Exhibit 5.2
Product Life Cycle: Stages and Characteristics

Characteristics	Introduction (Pioneering)	Growth (Acceptance)	Maturation (Saturation)	Decline (Obsolescence)
Sales	increasing slowly	increasing rapidly: later, more slowly	stable	decreasing permanently
Target Market	high income	middle income	mass market reached	low income
Competitors	very few direct competitors	highest	stable number	few small specialists
Product Modification	frequent	major	annual style change	few or none
Production & Marketing Costs	high for both	decreasing for both	stable for both	increasing production cost; declining marketing cost
Resistance to unfavorable Conditions	very poor	best	depending on economic conditions	product departure hastened
Trade-ins	none	few	many	few or none
Brand Loyalty	N/A	beginning to develop	strong	declining
Parts & Services Required	few parts but frequent services	large inventory	complex & costly	few
Profit	loss	good for both industry & firms	stable	reasonable for survivors

wallpaper blocked the radio signal, while the unit was often turned on by a vacuum cleaner or a lawn mower.

An innovative firm cannot cure these imperfections by waiting to introduce a new model the following year. As a result, product modification is usually immediate and frequent, being out of necessity and not of preference. Product services are thus critical, and the service network must be established. The inventory system, however, is relatively simple because a limited product line requires only a few parts to be stored.

While both frequent modifications and services contribute to high production costs, these are not the only reasons for high unit production cost. Other factors include the low production volume and a lack of specialized production equipment, resulting in inefficiency and diseconomies of scale. There is a parallel between production process and life cycle and PLC. A production process normally moves from a more flexible, inefficient, job-shop oriented method toward standardization and mechanization, which are less flexible and more capital-intensive.[3] Apparently, initial demand uncertainty necessitates the use of existing equipment rather than investing in new, specialized machinery.

The marketing costs, likewise, are also high because of the low sales volume and the need to attempt to change consumers' purchase habits and attitudes. Not surprisingly, a loss (rather than a profit) is the rule instead of an exception in the introduction stage. Time's *Sports Illustrated*, for example, did not yield any profit during its first ten years. As a matter of fact, if a product is introduced during a recession or at the time of other unfavorable economic conditions, its ability to overcome these negative factors is very low and its vulnerability toward failure is correspondingly high. The product could thus be done away with very easily, indicating the importance of giving extra attention to the timing of introduction.

Usually, products do not remain in the introductory stage for very long. The losses occurring in this stage make it imperative to move the product into the profitable growth stage as soon as possible. By the time most consumers are aware of their existence, most products would have already moved into the growth stage. Big-screen TV is one exception. Due to its high price, the product has still lingered in either the introductory stage or the slow growth stage even though it has been in the market for more than a decade.

GROWTH STAGE

The growth stage can be characterized by the product's market acceptance. Actually, this stage can be divided into two substages (as shown by the dotted line in Exhibit 5.1), because sales increase at an increasing rate (i.e., rapidly) in the first half of the growth stage while growing at decreasing rate (i.e., less rapidly) in the latter half of this stage. One example is the moderation of the growth rate of VCRs, signifying the movement from the first half to the second half of the growth stage. Compared with the previous year, the 1983 sales more than doubled. But the 1987 sales as compared to the volume of 1986 represented only a 2 percent increase because nearly two-thirds of U.S. households had already owned VCRs.

The increased sales volume now justifies the purchase of specialized equipment for production, which provides some improvement in economies of scale of production. Mass production, mass distribution, and mass marketing also bring about a drop in the costs of both production and marketing. The target market is shifted to the middle-income group in the first substage, with the lower-income consumers as the next target late in the growth stage (i.e., the second substage).

Unfortunately for the innovating firm, the number of competitors is at peak in this stage because opportunity-seeking firms are attracted by the product's profit potential and rush in to get a share of the market. After pioneering the low-price facsimile market in 1986, Sharp and Canon attracted more than 20 other competitors within just one year. Likewise, Apple Computer, once the only game in town, subsequently faced more than 150 competitors. Profit, however, is usually good for the industry as well as for each individual firm because of the strength of the market.

A severe shakeout eventually follows near the end of this stage because of the intense competition and extreme market requirements in terms of product assortment, parts, services, and price. Ultimately the strong firms do survive this stage to go on to the next stage.

Product modification is a fairly widespread activity because newcomers refine the existing product technology by adding innovative features, primarily for product differentiation. The few pioneering firms are thus forced to follow suit. In any case, it is reasonable to expect a significant product improvement. In 1987, for instance, manufacturers of satellite television equipment introduced the integrated receiver descrambler (IRD) which could revolutionize the industry. The component combines the functions of the satellite receiver, digital stereo sound, lock-out capabilities, and remote control. Previously, separate pieces at higher prices were necessary.

In addition to major improvements in the product, the market becomes segmented and is accompanied by several appropriate product models for each of these multiple segments. For example, video cassette recorders have changed greatly from their original one-hour recording capability to a single tape which can record for two hours, four hours, six hours, and now eight hours, and many versions of this product are equipped with such features as built-in timers, programmable capability, speed search, remote control, still frame, and so forth. Microwave ovens, likewise, have added trays, timers, browning units, convection cooking, and other special features.

Late in this stage as the product is nearing entry into the maturity stage, trade-in activity as well as brand loyalty commitment begin to surface because both retailers and consumers desire assurance of future parts and services. The inventories tend to become larger because of purchase volume and a deepening of the product line (i.e., multiple product models). This is the stage in which the product has the best chance of survival regardless of even adverse economic conditions because adjustments can be made in terms of lower price, simpler models, increased promotion, and so on in order to keep sales growing. Examples of products in this stage include video cassette recorders and microwave ovens. Microwave ovens have moved from the original segment of upscale suburban housewives. Aided by falling prices, the product has become a mass-market item.

Several products seem to have promising futures because their markets are not yet saturated, coupled with the fact that these products are affordable and appear to meet consumer needs. A study sponsored by the Electronics Industry Association revealed that telephone answering machines were in 24 percent of the homes, while personal computers and compact disk players had 18 percent and 14 percent respectively. For such products, the demand trends look favorable, and their sales are likely to grow.

MATURATION STAGE

The maturation or saturation stage can be characterized by a stable sales volume for the industry; in this stage all segments of the mass market are finally reached and saturated. Industry sales, however, are determined in part by economic conditions, because most households would have already purchased the product, and any replacement could be postponed should economic conditions not favor a replacement sale. Thus, sales would go up during good economic times and come down when times are depressed. The growth in the population alone cannot keep the market strong without the proper economic conditions and replacement demand.

To encourage replacement demand, many firms attempt to change their product styles annually. Such an adjustment in product in this day and age is likely to be more aesthetic than substantive, meaning that the modification is not likely to provide any significant change in the actual product performance. The strategy of deliberately making the old models obsolete by introducing a new annual style change is prevalent in the automobile industry. Textbook publishers likewise are able to disrupt the used-book market by introducing new editions every few years to make the previous editions obsolete. While it is debatable whether such planned obsolescence benefits the society or not, it is still a good marketing strategy because the product should be kept in the maturation stage as long as possible instead of letting it move into the decline stage.

Brand loyalty is another important factor, and if it is strong, it will help extend the maturation stage for a particular firm. As can be expected, trade-ins are also an important factor in the determination of company and industry sales volume as well as a determinant of maturity stage length.

The number of competitors is usually stable, with very few firms entering or leaving the industry. Calculators and watches are examples of mature businesses. At the peak, there were hundreds of competitors. Now only a handful of strong competitors remain.

The stable condition is caused by a number of entry barriers, consisting of a large stable sales volume, strong brand loyalty, established distribution network, and the full product line necessary in the highly segmented and highly competitive markets. Often a newcomer firm is hampered by the lack of economies of scale in production and marketing. Coupling this with a high initial investment, the venture becomes unreasonably risky. The oligopoly market situation is thus not uncommon within an industry existing in the maturity stage of the product life cycle.

Also, profit for each firm should be relatively constant, assuming that there is no significant improvement in the product. The inventory and service systems are likely to be complex and costly due to the sizable requirements brought about by the deep product line and annual style changes.

DECLINE STAGE

The decline stage, also known as product obsolescence, is the last stage. As implied by the name, sales are declining on a continual basis. The pace of the decline depends in part on how fast other new products enter the product life cycle and pass through their own cycle. Therefore, the cycle length varies from product to product. Exhibit 5.3 shows how the growth of plastic containers aids the decline of both glass and paper containers.

Just as sales decrease, trade-in activity, parts and services, and brand loyalty all decline in this stage. Furthermore, any adverse economic conditions will only serve to hasten the product's departure.

The automobile has been in the maturation stage for many decades. Whether it may enter the decline stage or not depends on whether a

Exhibit 5.3
Product Form Variations

milk container type	1967	1977	1987
glass	20%	1%	under .5%
paper	71%	58%	37%
plastic	7%	41%	63%

Source: Milk Industry Foundation, figures are rounded.

new, better, faster, and more economical mode of transportation is feasible. If objects and people could be beamed from place to place, automobiles and airplanes would have seen their better day.

The target group within this stage of the product life cycle is somewhat
difficult to generalize about. Early in the stage, it is most likely to be the
low-income group, whose members may finally get into the market.
Consumers in this group tend to be brand loyal, which makes these
customers enter and continue purchasing through most of this phase.
But late in the decline stage, the product may possibly become an antique
or a collector's item, which can then attract high-income customers.

Toward the end of the decline stage, only a few specialized firms
choose to remain in the market because it is so small and specialized,
making it financially unattractive for large firms or many firms to remain.
While product modification activity declines to almost nothing, the production costs do not decline any further. Actually, such costs begin to
increase again because of the lack of volume and the subsequent loss of
economies of scale.

The marketing costs, however, are likely to decline because of the lack
of competition and the needlessness of using mass media since it is
unnecessary to promote the product aggressively, if at all. Profit, while
small, is attractive for the remaining firms because of a shallow product
line, fewer parts and inventories, lack of competition, fewer retail outlets, brand loyalty among laggards, and inelastic demand.

Horse-drawn carriages and slide rules are examples of products existing very late in this stage, while black-and-white TV is in the early
part of the decline stage. Sophisticated hand-held calculators are in the
process of moving into this stage as well, if not already there, because
of the existence of portable and more powerful personal computers.

THEORETICAL SUPPORT FOR THE PLC CONCEPT

The reasons for the changes of a product through its life cycle are often not well understood. There are two critical underlying causes for the variations of product behavior during a cycle: instability of demand, and instability of supply (competitive position). Coincident with and contributing to an understanding to these two kinds of instability, there are two important theories: diffusion process of innovations theory (covered in chapter 4) and theory of monopolistic competition.

Diffusion theory seeks to explain the adoption of new products and services over time by consumers. In the introductory stage, a few persons (innovators) are purchasing the product. If the product is successful, more buyers (early adopters) will come into the market, causing a rapid growth in sales in the first half of the growth stage. A large number of buyers will follow (early majority), explaining the increase in sales in the second half of the same growth stage. Interaction and imitation among consumers cause more people to follow early buyers in purchasing the product. The sales in the maturation stage become relatively stable with the support of the next group (late majority) before declining and attracting the last group of buyers (laggards) in the decline stage.

The second underlying theory that helps explain the behavior of the product life cycle is Chamberlin's theory of monopolistic competition. Monopolistic competition is a market structure in which there are many firms selling products which are close, but not perfect, substitutes for each other. Because of the lack of market entry barriers, market prosperity will quickly attract new competitors. To compete, both the established and the new firms tend to use product differentiation to gain strategic advantage. The product's psychological function is thus as important as its engineering aspect. But when the market collapses, many competitors will hastily exit. Therefore, the theory of monopolistic competition provides a rationale for the variation in the number of firms and their behavior in the different stages of the PLC.

EMPIRICAL EVIDENCE

Empirically, one study found that the time span from rapid growth to maturity is more than 40 years for many industrial products.[4] For most product types, however, the duration of the life cycle is becoming shorter due to the increasing pace of technological innovation and the rapid rate of new product introduction.[5] In another study, PLC curves were found to exist for more than 80 percent of the products investigated.[6] But unlike the classical bell curve, there are sharp changes from stage to stage, and the turning points are not clearly identifiable.

Product life cycle has been criticized for being ambiguous and difficult to measure in addition to having a low predictive value and for being inapplicable to many products that are exceptions and do not behave as suggested. As a matter of fact, the classical and familiar PLC curve is only one of 12 possible pattern types.[7]

There will always be some products which largely conform to the described PLC phenomenon as well as others which will contradict it. Time's SAMI study illustrates this point well.[8] Graphing sales against time frames of four weeks for grocery products introduced in the early 1970s and sold for at least five years, product life cycles were found for more than 80 percent of such products. Furthermore, sales peaks for 60 percent of these products were never exceeded or matched at a later stage, indicating that the marketing mix cannot reverse a declining trend. On the other hand, the curves found, while predictable, were different from the bell-jar curve, and the peaks and valleys during the maturity stage confirm the influence of promotional efforts.

EXCEPTIONS

As stated earlier, there are many products which do not go through a product life cycle. A product may start out so strongly that it does not even go through a period of slow growth. Fashions and fads are prime examples of products that behave in this manner in the marketplace. Videogame cartridges are another example. Many games peaked in popularity within weeks of introduction. As a matter of fact, the total market for video games, after peaking at $3 billion in sales in 1982, completely and quickly collapsed and dragged the sales volume down to a mere $100 million in 1985.

In contrast, some products may go directly into the decline stage without going through the maturity stage. Once again, fashion and fads are examples of this process. The sales of Charlie's Angels dolls took a nosedive when the TV series was cancelled.

On the other hand, there are many products which never move past the introductory stage (e.g., midi skirts). Many others do not go beyond their test marketing period (e.g., Procter & Gamble's wet toilet paper).

Another exception may occur when a declining or mature product reenters the growth stage. Although having been in the market for several decades, Salem still has performed very well. In 1985, it was the world's fastest growing menthol brand and among the fastest growing of all cigarette categories. Camel, first introduced in 1913, was the fastest growing brand in the early 1980s—thanks to overseas sales. In the same period, Barbie dolls had a sales volume which was the best since 1959. G.I. Joe toys, which suffered during the Carter administration, made a strong comeback when Ronald Reagan became president.

Another good example of a product which is experiencing regrowth is the television industry, due in large part to recent technological and social trends. Home entertainment has become popular once again, and many new entertainment products can be plugged into a TV set, for example, VCRs, videodisc players, video games, TV cameras, satellite antennas, home computers, hi-fi sound, cable TV, and two-way communications or telephones. Such new devices will undoubtedly encourage people to buy more TV sets and/or to trade in their aging sets. Sony projects that for every four to five VCRs sold, another TV set is purchased. As a result, the market saturation level for television sets must be redefined. Even though 99 percent of all households have at least one TV set, with 35 percent having three or more TV sets, the saturation definition now means one TV set per person rather than one for each household.

A product can make a comeback. Let's consider Bausch & Lomb's black-framed, green-lensed Wayfarers, which is a style of chunky Ray-Ban sunglasses. Introduced in 1953, the sales peaked at 300,000 in the early 1960s and declined to 18,000 by 1981 due to the popularity of metal frames. Luckily, *Gentlemen's Quarterly* magazine showed their models using Wayfarers in 1982, followed by newspapers and such magazines as *Cosmopolitan, Glamour, New Yorker, Harper's Bazaar*, and *Mademoiselle*, coupled with Tom Cruise's appearance with them in the movie *Risky Business*. From the death bed to a fad all over again, sales climbed back to the level achieved during the peak period.

Fountain pens likewise have made a miraculous recovery. They offer comfortable writing without pressure. Just as important is the fact that the nib wears over time to the unique grip and angle of the hand, making it a handcrafted item which gives a person a sense of control.

A CONTROVERSY: DOUBTERS AND BELIEVERS

Product life cycle is a popular concept which has generated a great deal of discussion and enthusiasm among marketing scholars and marketing students. It is debatable, however, whether the concept generates the same kind of excitement among marketing practitioners. The concept has sometimes been criticized by marketing scholars, who raise questions concerning the validity of the PLC concept. Yet in most cases, these same scholars do not offer solutions or suggestions that may help in establishing the soundness of the concept.

A Charge

Do products behave in the patterns suggested by PLC? One study compared the predictions made by the PLC hypotheses with those of-

fered by random numbers generated over the same length of time.[9] Of more than 100 product categories, only 17 percent of product classes and 20 percent of product forms significantly differed from the random behavior (i.e., chance) generated in an artificial market. As may be expected, there was even less validity for product brands.

Based on the movement of product forms and product brands, while some products declined, others went in the opposite direction. Marlboro, once behind Winston, is now the solid number one cigarette, after unseating Winston, the former leader, several years ago. Of course, if products were expected to behave as described by PLC, all of them would have been expected to go in the same direction, probably at the same pace, within the same period of time. Therefore, product life cycle, usually perceived as an independent variable which influences the marketing mix, functions in exactly the opposite direction and is a dependent variable whose behavior depends on the marketing mix, not vice versa.

If a marketer believes that his product is entering the decline stage, he may be tempted to withdraw his support from that product. The product in fact, through no fault of its own, may be doing poorly because of poor advertising or severe competition. Any further neglect as suggested by PLC would simply and surely do away with the product once and for all, resulting in a self-fulfilling prophecy according to the strategy suggested by the product life cycle.

The aspects mentioned may thus cast some doubt on the reliability of PLC. Based on these criticisms, some marketers advise that it is impractical to adjust the marketing mix to fit a particular stage since the stage that the product is in is often influenced by the marketing mix.

A Countercharge

Some scholars take the opposite view, disagreeing with those who have questioned the usefulness of the PLC concept. With regard to the allegation that PLC fails to consider competition and marketing activities, this charge is pure nonsense. After all, the primary reason for studying PLC in the first place is that the varying competitive environment from stage to stage necessitates adjustments in marketing strategies.

Several scholars refuse to allow that the product life cycle may in fact be a dependent variable. If a product is indeed dying and the marketer still refuses to give it up, many marketers see any further support for the product as a case of pouring good money after bad money in a futile effort to revive a hopeless situation. What should be realized is that a continuance of support for the dying product is likely to cut off any opportunity for the creation of product spin-offs and the support necessary to nurture them. Subsequently, not only is the declining product eliminated, but any chance for the development of new fresh products

is virtually eliminated—much like throwing the baby out with the dirty water. Based on this rationale, PLC must be considered an independent variable, and this consideration should be used to guide the implementation of the appropriate marketing strategies.

A Compromise

Admittedly, these two views, though poles apart, do have their individual merits. However, it may be impossible and not worth the effort to determine if PLC is a dependent or independent variable. The same thing may also be said about the marketing mix. Moreover, it may not matter to a significant degree whether PLC and marketing mix are independent variables. What is important is that they are closely associated, and a change in one will profoundly affect the other. If the product is maturing, the marketing mix must be adjusted to be consistent with the product characteristics in that stage. On the other hand, if there is a chance that an old product can be revitalized, then the utilization of the marketing mix must be the means to bring it from decline. Of course, if the revitalization process is not effective, then a decision must be made to eliminate the product from the product line.

Though product life cycle analysis does provide a basis for product analysis, the concept should not be taken in blind faith and treated as a substitute for logical judgment. It may be true that a good deal of subjectivity can be involved in judgment, and this complicates the process of making a wise decision. But if logical judgment is combined with an appreciation for the information provided in the product life cycle concept, a better market decision should be the result of the interactive process between the marketing mix and the product life cycle.

THE MARKETING MIX

Many criticisms of PLC are somewhat unfair. If the PLC concept has any fault, it is not so much that of ignoring the competitive environment but rather that of not adequately or explicitly spelling out the competitive factors. Actually, the main reason for studying PLC in the first place is the necessity of adjusting the marketing effort to conform to the changing environment. It is foolish to believe that the life cycle of any given product can be indefinitely extended. Once the product is obsolete, any extravagant marketing effort is not going to bring about its reincarnation. It is difficult to envision how marketing efforts can rejuvenate the sales of slide rules or horse-drawn carriages. Thus to overlook the necessity of matching the marketing mix to product life cycle stages is to invite unnecessary difficulties.

It is unfortunate that the controversy about whether or not PLC is an independent variable seems to cloud the real issue of the practical value of the concept. The truth of the matter is that it does not matter whether the marketing mix and product life cycle stages are independent variables or not, because the influence of each upon the other is definitely not unilateral. Both of these concepts are so interdependent that they cannot avoid influencing each other. They must thus be considered simultaneously when formulating marketing strategy and not as independent functions.

Parker Brothers's diversification from the toy business into children's books illustrates how the marketing mix was considered. The company's "product" strategy was to create a product rather than a commodity. It thus created Care Bears, a family of ten cute bears, each having a distinct symbol and personality (e.g., Tenderheart Bear with a red heart on its protruding tummy). Parker Brothers, wanting these bears to teach children about changing emotions, used marketing research to identify popular story lines.

Parker Brothers was quite aggressive in promoting the Care Bears books. It spent $1 million on a half-hour TV special to promote the product concept. The amount was considered aggressive in light of the industry's annual advertising expenditures of less than $3 million. With this unique concept and hefty promotion, the company was able to charge a premium price for the hardcover series. In terms of distribution, the company planned to use a channel which was not considered by competitors—toy and discount stores. Book stores were de-emphasized, and no exchange or return of unsold books was allowed.

An understanding of product life cycle and its stages makes it possible for the marketer to adjust his marketing mix variables so that they are consistent with a particular stage within which his product may be found. While it is impractical to believe that a universal solution can be offered for all types of products, it is still useful to provide a framework consisting of general strategies concerning the four Ps of marketing. Exhibit 5.4 shows the necessary adjustments in the marketing mix variables for the four PLC stages.

INTRODUCTION STRATEGIES

A wise marketer's strategy in the *introduction* stage is to provide the market with only one or a very few product models. A limited product line policy is justified because the marketer should go after the total market rather than trying to segment the market. The number of distribution or retail outlets is usually minimal because the product is a specialty one, making widespread distribution not yet necessary. Sony initially treated its compact disc player as a specialty good and limited the distribution to only specialty stores. Magnavox, in contrast, did not

Exhibit 5.4
Product Life Cycle: Marketing Mix

Characteristics	Introduction (Pioneering)	Growth (Acceptance)	Maturation (Saturation)	Decline (Obsolescence)
Product	shallow product line	deeper product line (i.e., seg-mentation)	deepest line (highly segmented market)	shallow product line
Place (Distribution)	exclusive	selective	intensive	selective
Promotion	primary demand	selective demand	selective demand	primary demand
Price	highest	declining	stable	declining, then stable, and probably increasing later

fare as well. It chose department stores as its distribution network, aiming at the mass market too soon. To compound the problem, Magnavox offered more than one version of the product, needlessly confusing potential buyers, who had to be educated.

The promotional appeal must be based on a primary demand basis (i.e., product class or product form advertising) without too much concern for selective demand cultivation (i.e., brand advertising). This promotional tactic is warranted because there are only a few competitors to contend with and it is more important for the basic product rather than particular brands to gain market acceptance. If the product succeeds, all pioneering brands have an excellent chance at success. If it fails, none of the brands in the market will matter anyway.

If the few brands in the market of the same product are based on different and incompatible systems, the firms must aggressively market its own system in order to become the industry standard. This strategy is highly recommended because if other systems are accepted, the company's substantial investment will become worthless, not to mention the fact that the company will even have to convert its product to fit its rival's system. As a further point, the availability of many systems serves only to confuse consumers at this early stage and consequently is likely to retard sales growth. One reason why the 4-channel sound product failed was that there were too many competing systems.

In regard to price, it should be set high and most likely will be highest of all stages due to several contributing factors: low sales, frequent product modifications, high production and marketing costs, uncertainty of product success, desire to recoup research and development costs as soon as possible, and desire to keep demand within the company's production capacity.

GROWTH STRATEGIES

In the *growth* stage, more competitors enter, and their aggressive tactics make it impossible for the market to remain unsegmented any longer. Multiple product models must be developed to adapt to these changes. Sharp and Canon initially used low-cost facsimile machines to cultivate the fax market. Once the market was established, they began to offer more expensive models with more capabilities. For example, their top-end machines have multiple-page document feeders and can be programmed to send stacks of documents at night.

The product line expansion is necessary to keep distributors and/or retailers satisfied by making them competitive and profitable in the battle to increase or maintain market share. Distributor loyalty is important in light of the fact that the number of distribution outlets will grow rapidly as newcomers want exposure for their products and pioneering firms want to expand their markets. After all, retailers have shelf space for only a few brands.

Market segmentation and product line expansion should also be used with service businesses in the maturity stage. Based on the 1980 census, one-fifth of those who are fifteen years old or older (or 35 million people) have some physical impairment. Airlines could create brand loyalty if only they would become sensitive to the needs of this market segment. Facilities should be made more accessible. For example, a lavatory should have an oversized door and increased floor space without any bump or ridge that wheelchairs must go over. In addition to installations of necessary apparatus, appropriate attitudes must be instilled. That is, it is important to sensitize employees.

The credit card business is also a mature industry. Following the script of the PLC theory, credit card issuers have turned to market segmentation. The market is now segmented in numerous ways. One of the recent marketing practices is affinity cards which are sponsored by religious, charitable, educational, or social organizations. These cards bear emblem of a labor union, college, or club. Citibank even allows its Visa cardholders to have cards with pictures of the helmets of their favorite National Football League teams. Other cards have airline affiliations (e.g., Mileage Plus Visa card issued by First National Bank of Chicago and United Airlines) that enable users to collect frequent flyer points every time they use the cards. First National Bank of Wilmington, on the other hand, goes after educators with its "educator advantage" program which offers, among other things, educators-only interest rebate and educators-only two-month summer "skip payment" option.

By the same rationale, price must be adjusted downward, especially with more sales, less frequent product modification, the target group consisting of middle-income consumers, and increases in production time and efficiency, all of which exert an immense pressure on price. As shown in the case of video game machines and video games near the end of the growth stage, these items were sold at prices which hardly yielded any profit.

Selective demand promotion, of course, is now the appropriate strategy to counter more competition. Most firms tend to differentiate their brands through advertising as well as by adding unique product features. Nonetheless, a market leader can continue to combine both primary demand and selective demand in his advertising because he is assured of a large proportion of any increase in demand.

MATURATION STRATEGIES

Only the strong firms remain to survive in the *maturation* stage, especially when the market is highly segmented. The intense competition makes it almost imperative that the company must have a complete product line—a separate model for each segment—in order to remain powerful and maintain its market share. The U.S. automobile market has 163 car models. According to J. D. Power & Associates, an auto mobile marketing research firm, the number of models is expected to reach 235 in 1992.

Distributors must be carefully selected and trained, because the firm's success is largely a function of dealer strength and cooperation. A strong distribution network of loyal and competent members can provide a competitive advantage.

The changing marketing mix further requires that the company promote its product on the selective demand basis, possibly with varying appeals for each market segment. Let's consider orange juice as an example. Two major problems of orange juice are that it is a mature business and that consumers treat it as a commodity, buying whatever brand is on sale. To solve these problems, Coca-Cola's Minute Maid, Procter & Gamble's Citrus Hill, and Beatrice's Tropicana all wanted to convince buyers that orange juice brands were not created equal. To achieve their goal, they borrowed the tactic from marketers of detergents and soft drinks—segmenting the market and offering new products for the various segments. Tropicana, at one time, had Pure Premium as the only chilled juice not made from concentrate. Minute Maid countered with the Country Style version containing bits of orange pulp, in addition to another product that was sweeter and had reduced acid. Minute Maid's line extension included Squeeze Fresh frozen concentrate in a squeezable bottle to allow consumers to make one glass of orange juice at a time. Procter & Gamble used the health approach and endorsement, a page borrowed from the marketing of its Crest toothpaste. Citrus Hill Plus Calcium was endorsed by the American Women's Medical Association since most people do not get enough calcium. Another one of its product forms was Lite Citrus Hill which was a low-calorie 60 percent juice.

One exception to the rule of primary demand promotion in the maturity stage is the case of substitutable commodities. Primary demand promotion must be used in the maturity stage because the competition is at the product class level. The aim is to take market share from other product classes (competitors).

The promotion of primary demand or product class (and product form to a lesser extent) is best illustrated by meat producers, who all attempt to convince consumers to choose their meat over other kinds of meat. After all, consumers can only eat so much and do have many meat varieties for selection.

Beef, once having a sovereign place at the dinner table, for a long time received no marketing support. Now, to fend off other alternatives, beef producers used James Garner in the "real meat for real people" campaign. The threat to beef comes from several fronts. Poultry provides a low-cost alternative. The American Lamb Council has repositioned lamb as "a food that fits into today's lifestyle" by calling it the "lean, light, luscious, limitless American lamb."

Pork producers have waged a fierce campaign. The National Pork Products Council (NPPC) found in 1980 that 40 percent of consumers were light eaters or nonusers of pork due to negative perceptions: pork was too fatty and greasy and took too long to cook to prevent health hazards. The NPPC has thus mandated a legislative national checkoff among pork producers. The money collected, .25 percent for each hog sold, was used to reposition pork as "the other white meat" to capitalize on the trend toward moving away from red meat. To educate consumers of pork's positive attributes (low levels of calorie and cholesterol), the NPPC devised the "America is leaning on pork" campaign. To promote pork for year-round consumption, the NPPC used: (1) "warm up to pork" to promote pork chops, roast, and ham dishes in the summer, (2) "fall for porkfest" to show ways to cook ribs, roasts, and chops in autumn, and (3) "season's treatings" to demonstrate the versatility of chops, crown roast, ham, and sausages for winter.

Much like the other variables in this "stable" stage, price should be kept stable. This does not mean that price cannot be increased; it is still regarded as stable as long as it increases in the same proportion as inflation. Automobile prices over the past two decades have largely performed in this fashion and are an example of this practice.

In any case, if it is feasible, all firms should compete on a nonprice basis because any price cut simply erodes the profit margin for all firms with no significant gain in market share for anyone. This problem is well illustrated by the television industry: Zenith and RCA both want to be number one, and this has resulted in a price war between themselves, the Japanese products, and other foreign competitors. The final effect of this price competition is that a severe profit squeeze currently exists within this industry.

DECLINE STRATEGIES

The marketing mix will have to be adjusted once again in the final stage of *decline*. Promotion should be directed toward primary demand in order to slow down the sales decline through the use of narrow, selective (not mass) media. Product lines should be reduced because market segmentation is no longer a necessity. This does not mean that a declining product should be automatically deleted, but instead that a product should be retained as long as it still contributes something to the firm's overall fixed costs. Also, any product withdrawal should not be so abrupt as to leave distributors and customers vulnerable; otherwise, hard-earned good will and future cooperation may be lost.

Not only will customers have to come to expect less product selection but they will also have to expect a limited availability of distribution outlets—the product now takes on some of the qualities of a specialty good, with exposure somewhat unimportant and inconvenience expected. Price will go through several stages—declining at the beginning, becoming stable later on, and probably rising again due to lower sales volume and the factor of inelastic demand.

CONCLUSION

People, seasons, and products, among others things, change as they go through time. According to the PLC concept, a product usually advances through four stages: introduction, growth, maturation, and decline. During the company life cycle, sales, profits, consumers, competitors, and so on all change continuously, and such changes are explained in part by the diffusion process of innovations theory and the theory of monopolistic competition, which are concerned with changes that occur due to demand and supply in the marketplace.

One criticism of the PLC concept is aimed at the treatment of PLC as an independent variable that influences the marketing mix. According to these critics, PLC is actually a dependent variable whose cycle is determined by the marketing mix. This allegation lacks merit on two counts. First, the premise of the criticism rests on a selling orientation, long discredited by virtually all marketing scholars, which assumes that anything can be sold regardless of suitability as long as it is pushed aggressively enough. Second, the issue of whether PLC is an independent variable or not is an empty debate, not unlike the futile attempt to determine whether the chicken or the egg came first. It is a waste of effort to argue for a causal relationship when the establishment of mere association is adequate. It is more fruitful to acknowledge the fact that PLC and the marketing mix are highly interdependent.

PLC should not be used in place of the marketing manager's judgment. What PLC can do is to make the manager aware of the competitive changes so that adjustments can be made in marketing strategies. The consideration of PLC can also raise important and interesting questions that can be useful in providing a framework for marketing implementation.

As far as the marketer is concerned, it is critical for him to understand the changing competitive environment so that he can adjust his marketing mix (i.e., product, place, promotion, and price) accordingly. The PLC concept provides generalizations in regard to the proper application of the four Ps of marketing. However, it is not possible for the marketing mix to be applicable for all products under all circumstances. But then again, no one single theory could be expected to do so anyway.

An analysis and application of the concepts of the product life cycle and the marketing mix is not likely to be a panacea for all. It would be naive to believe that the road to success is achieved by simply examining PLC and its suggestions. A better way to visualize the PLC would be to realize what it can do in providing a framework for understanding the behavior of products and competitive conditions and then to make management aware of these circumstances. In the balance, however, human judgment is still needed, and it is the marketing manager's function to evaluate and select the best avenue for determining problems and opportunities pointed out by the PLC concept.

NOTES

1. Joe Agnew, "Marketers Serve Up Low-Salt Products as Consumers Shed Their Sodium Habit," *Marketing News*, 28 March 1988, pp. 1–2.

2. Thomas A. Staudt, Donald A. Taylor, and Donald J. Bowersox, *A Managerial Introduction to Marketing*, 3rd ed. (Englewood Cliffs, N.J.: Prentice-Hall, 1976) pp. 221–45.

3. Robert H. Hayes and Steven C. Wheelwright, "Link Manufacturing Process and Product Life Cycles," *Harvard Business Review* 57 (January-February 1979): 133–40.

4. Hans B. Thorelli and Stephen C. Burnett, "The Nature of Product Life Cycles for Industrial Goods," *Journal of Marketing* 45 (Fall 1981): 97–108.

5. William Qualls, Richard W. Olshavsky, and Ronald E. Michaels, "Short-

ening of the PLC—An Empirical Test," *Journal of Marketing* 45 (Fall 1981): 76–80.

6. "Grocery Products Exhibit Different Life Cycle Curve," *Marketing News*, 6 August 1982, p. 6.

7. David R. Rink and John E. Swan, "Product Life Cycle Research: A Literature Review," *Journal of Business Research* 78 (September 1979): 219–42.

8. "Grocery Products," p. 6.

9. Nariman K. Dhalla and Sonia Uyspeh, "Forget the Product Life Cycle Concept," *Harvard Business Review* 54 (January-February 1976): 102–12.

6

Product Life Cycle: Other Competitive Strategies

PLC: NOT FOR THEORISTS ONLY

It is a foregone conclusion that marketing educators and students alike are highly familiar with the product life cycle (PLC) concept. After all, the concept is the pride and joy of the marketing discipline. The value of the PLC concept lies in its simplicity and straightforward nature coupled with the practical implications for strategic product management. As explained by an executive vice president of Gillette (North America), "The number of entrants in a given category has increased, and we find ourselves really working hard at projecting a given brand's life cycle—when the bell curve is likely to peak and the point at which it is no longer intelligent to support a given brand."

Since PLC curves do exist and have strategic implications, why then does active use of the PLC stop at the classroom door? Why do business graduates leave it behind, with their caps, gowns, and other academic baggage? Is the theory really only another memento of their college years, or does it have practical relevance in a practical corporate world?

This chapter examines the practical role of PLC in the competitive corporate setting. It suggests a number of strategies that business persons can use. The chapter will also evaluate marketing strategies that can be employed by business firms to gain a differential advantage within the competitive environment of the PLC.

RIDING THE PLC

Some believe that management will do what it wants to with a product without regard to the stage the product is in in the life cycle. This charge is only partially valid since it ignores the fact that sound management practice is based on scientific knowledge. Anyone, of course, can ignore anything. But an intelligent corporate leader would be foolish not to consider a good theory which can help improve the company's profitability.

A company can ignore the implications of PLC at its own peril. For too long, AT&T thrived under the protection of monopolistic regulations and saw no need to upgrade its standard black telephone. This is very surprising given the fact that its Bell Labs are considered to be the most productive research and development organization in the world. It is doubtful that the company can continue to be successful in the more competitive environment without learning the need to shorten the life cycle of its obsolete products. IBM's success can be attributed in part to its deliberate attempt to continuously shorten the life cycle of its products by ceaseless innovation. On average, IBM's main computer systems go through a total change every six years. It was thus very uncharacteristic of IBM to wait so long to upgrade its personal computers (PCs) while its competitors were making successful strategy modifications appropriate for this product's life cycle stage.

How can managerial action mitigate competitive effects as a product moves through its life cycle? The following sections discuss how PLC provides a framework of general strategies for modifying product, place (distribution), pricing, and promotion to make them compatible with the particular stage of a product (see Exhibits 6.1 and 6.2).[1]

"FISH WHERE THE FISH ARE"—AN IMITATION STRATEGY

It is far easier for a new product to fail than to succeed. Given the generally poor survival record of new products along with the huge investment associated with their introduction, there is great risk in playing pioneer. Not surprisingly, many companies deliberately avoid being first in the market. Hiram Walker's policy, for example, is to "fish where the fish are." The company prefers to see other firms enter and test new markets first before moving in quickly when the demand is solidly in place.[2]

To imitate is one thing, but to do it well is another matter. It is not enough just to be an imitator; one must also learn to be an *effective* imitator. Generally, a good imitator is a fast one. This was exactly the problem faced by Procter & Gamble's Duncan Hines crisp and chewy chocolate chip cookies, which use two separate doughs. The successful test marketing of the product did not result in national distribution for more than a year. By that time, however, Nabisco and Keebler were already in the market with their own versions. The same pattern may well apply to IBM. Now that Big Blue has introduced its new Personal System/2 PCs, clone makers are busy trying to duplicate the operating system and beat each other to the market with their IBM-compatible machines. To succeed, however, they must copy not only well, but quickly.

Another entry strategy for latecomers involves using brand extensions. By extending an established and popular name to a new product, a company can minimize the strategic advantage of the first entrant. Tide, for example, although being quite late for the liquid detergent segment, was able to capitalize on its name successfully for its Liquid Tide detergent.

Marketers who are slow in entering a market will find it doubly locked away, both by innovators and fast imitators. To thrive, a slow imitator must therefore change several rules of the game. One way of doing so is to offer a significantly improved version of the earlier (pioneer) product, so that some kind of product differentiation is achieved. Mattel, for instance, lost $361 million in its home computer venture because its machine, as a latecomer, was just another me-too product. Osborne, in contrast, was a successful pioneer of the bundling of computer hardware and software until it was beaten at its own game by Kaypro's significant

Exhibit 6.1
In Search of a Strategic Advantage

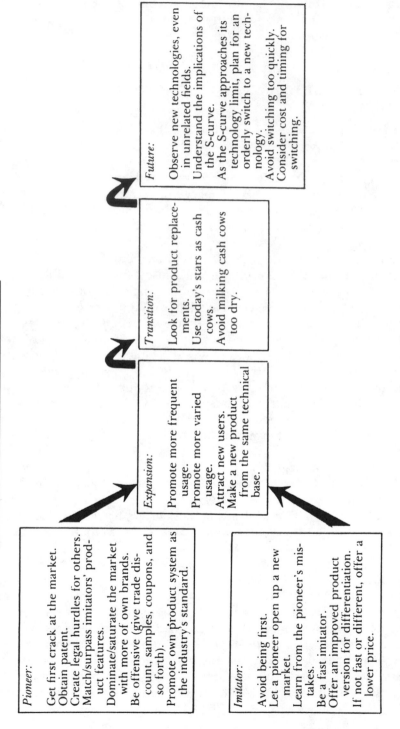

Pioneer:

Get first crack at the market.
Obtain patent.
Create legal hurdles for others.
Match/surpass imitators' product features.
Dominate/saturate the market with more of own brands.
Be offensive (give trade discount, samples, coupons, and so forth).
Promote own product system as the industry's standard.

Imitator:

Avoid being first.
Let a pioneer open up a new market.
Learn from the pioneer's mistakes.
Be a fast imitator.
Offer an improved product version for differentiation.
If not fast or different, offer a lower price.

Expansion:

Promote more frequent usage.
Promote more varied usage.
Attract new users.
Make a new product from the same technical base.

Transition:

Look for product replacements.
Use today's stars as cash cows.
Avoid milking cash cows too dry.

Future:

Observe new technologies, even in unrelated fields.
Understand the implications of the S-curve.
As the S-curve approaches its technology limit, plan for an orderly switch to a new technology.
Avoid switching too quickly.
Consider cost and timing for switching.

Source: Adapted from Sak Onkvisit and John J. Shaw, "Competition and Product Management: Can the Product Life Cycle Help?" *Business Horizons* 29 (July/August 1986): 55.

Exhibit 6.2
PLC and Marketing Strategies

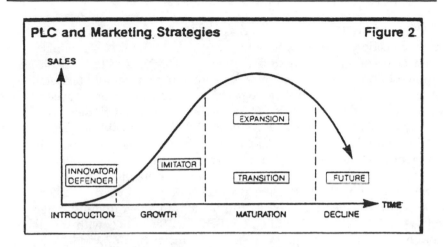

improvement. Osborne's five-inch monitor with a 52-column screen was no match for Kaypro's nine-inch monitor with an 80-column screen.

The success of the Compaq Portable was due to more than its IBM compatibility. Compaq offered, for less money, several more built-in features such as extra memory, two floppy disk drives, monochrome screen, color card, and printer port.

Those imitators who are neither fast nor unique must pay a penalty; they must offer the consumer lower prices. Notwithstanding, even penalties can be transformed into a differential advantage. Consider Hyundai, for example: Although late in entering the U.S. market, it has been able to overcome this handicap by selling its cars and Blue Chip PCs at prices aimed at the lowest segment of the market.

"PROTECT YOUR OWN TURF"—A DEFENSIVE STRATEGY

It is disheartening for a pioneer to persevere only to see imitators exploit the fruits of its labor. Pillsbury's experience with its new cake mix, Pillsbury Plus, is a good illustration. The cake mix quickly became the number one seller. It was so successful that the company was able to increase its market share to 21 percent. But Pillsbury Plus soon fell to the number three slot when General Mills and Procter & Gamble offered similar products and outperformed Pillsbury because of its relatively small position in the food industry.

Minnetonka's unfortunate experience in pioneering the liquid soap segment is another example. Because of its small size, the company was unable to protect its own turf. Before long, its Softsoap was replaced as a leader of liquid soaps by Procter & Gamble's Ivory Liquid.

The Pillsbury Plus and Softsoap examples make it clear that a pioneer must consider in advance how to protect itself should its product succeed. Toward this goal, there are several strategies which can be implemented to turn back challengers. As a start, patents should be obtained whenever possible, since the legal barriers can block or at least slow down the competition. This is how Polaroid removed Kodak from the instant photography market. Likewise, Hybritech was able to file patent-infringement lawsuits and obtain a preliminary injunction to bar Abbott Laboratories from selling diagnostic tests based on the so-called sandwich assay method, which uses monoclonal antibodies.

Similarly, in its haste to enter the PC market, IBM used readily available parts which could be easily duplicated, in effect inviting others to follow suit. In contrast, IBM's new Personal System/2, with the micro channel, reflects a change in strategy. To make cloning more difficult, IBM tried to obtain as many as 100 patents on its new computers. The lesson seems clear: He who litigates is rarely lost.

The OS/2 computer system demonstrates what the innovator and imitators must do. IBM repeatedly announced that it would sue anyone who infringed upon its OS/2's many patents. To acquire proof of infringement, IBM incorporated certain tests into its PS/2 computers' BIOS (Basic Input/Output System). BIOS is a software on a computer chip (i.e., a program linking a computer's software to hardware). IBM planned to perform these tests on any imitation. The legal uncertainty made BIOS designers and clonemakers hesitate to offer clones and retailers reluctant to carry them. IBM even filed a lawsuit against AST Research for its advertising message—"PS/2 Memory. Our name says it all"—promoting AST's products for use with IBM's PS/2. AST, although finally agreeing to modify its message, paid no damages and continued to use the "/2" suffix.

Phoenix Technologies, aware of the PS/2 potential and legal complications, was very careful in designing BIOS for clonemakers. It documented every step of its product design to prevent the problem of copyright infringement. Phoenix used one team of engineers to take apart the new IBM machines. This team then came up with a set of specifications to be given to another team of "clean" engineers to write the final software. Since the "clean" team never saw the IBM product, it could claim that there was no copying.

After steadfastly refusing to let others use its PS/2 technology, IBM finally made an announcement in 1988, a year after the introduction of PS/2, that it would allow other companies to create clones. This change of heart does not seem like an accident or an about-face. First, IBM understood that for its OS/2 system to become the industry standard, there must be clones to make the system respectable and to legitimize it. Second, with or without IBM's approval, efforts like that of Phoenix Technologies were bound to succeed. It thus would be better for IBM to collect royalties. After all, this provides extra revenue while increasing costs for competitors.

IBM's delay in making the licensing announcement created market uncertainty, which allowed the company to ask for a hefty royalty (as high as 5 percent of sales instead of the previous 1 percent). Also, the deliberate delay caused competitors to lag behind in developing similar products. This gave IBM extra time to take advantage of its technology. As explained by IBM's senior vice president, "All you can expect with technical innovation is to remain 12 to 14 months ahead." One of IBM's engineers made a comment along the same line: "By the time they can screw together a system that resembles Micro Channel, we'll have made improvements in it."

Another effective strategy is to strike preemptively by lowering price to maintain market share as well as economies of scale. This action, in effect, should convince potential competitors that the profit margin is not that attractive. IBM, for example, stays competitive and keeps its competitors on guard by periodically cutting prices on its various products. In the case of the IBM PC system, the prices were as follows: August 1981 introduction ($5,455), May 1982 ($4,745), July 1982 ($4,175), August 1982 ($3,940), March 1983 ($3,339), June 1984 ($2,580), and April 1985 ($2,064).

Generally, the price of a new product should be kept high initially due to a number of reasons—limited supply, product uniqueness, high production and marketing costs, and limited competition. As these conditions subsequently change, the price must be lowered. The lowering of the price should be anticipated and planned rather than being taken as a result of following competitors' actions. A company should act rather than react; it should beat the imitators to the punch.

Cannon gained a technological edge initially with its lush new twist-less yarn for its Royal Touch towel. When other mills introduced the same yarn, Cannon responded by dropping its wholesale price from $8 to $5. This pricing strategy was preceded by having capital improvement and large, efficient facilities. This move made it difficult for others to match Cannon's price cut without squeezing margins.

Texas Instruments has finally learned to price according to supply and value. The company is now not afraid to demand a premium price for a product that has a technological advantage. When the demand for its Speak and Spell far exceeded the capacity, the price was increased by 36 percent. Once the technological edge was gone, Texas Instruments maintained the premium price by relying on its brand name and reputation.

For the pioneer to come up with good defensive tactics, it should think like its imitators. It can frustrate competitors by assuming the imitator role itself. One strategy is for the innovator to saturate the new market with more of its own brands, making it too crowded for anybody else to enter and leaving no retail shelf space for potential competitors. Procter & Gamble, for example, added Luvs to join Pampers in its disposable diaper line. It could, of course, add a third variant and many others.

Kraft, learning from its research of high consumer interest in a stronger, spicier barbecue sauce, decided to introduce Bull's-Eye with a "big bold taste." The strategy was risky because it could have damaged the Kraft brand, which had dominated the barbecue sauce market with a 50 precent market share. Yet Kraft had the courage to risk attacking itself to prevent Heinz or Open Pit from cultivating the premium segment. The bold strategy paid off, with Bull's-Eye expanding the company's barbecue sauce franchise by 25 percent.

Imitators grow discouraged if the pioneer can match or surpass their product features. A competitor's potential imitation strategy may then become too risky because the imitated versions become obsolete. Procter & Gamble, creator of the disposable diaper market, was so dominant at one time that it lost sight of competition. After being stung by Kimberly-Clark's Huggies and its contoured model, Procter & Gamble's Pampers was able to regain market share only after spending $500 million for the equipment to make shaped and improved diapers. Its Ultra Pampers is a superabsorbent diaper whose inner core is made of wood pulp and a water-absorbing polymer that turns to a gel when wet. As advertised by Procter & Gamble, Ultra Pampers' superior advantages are: "ultra absorbent, ultra dry, and ultra thin."

Sony's experience with Walkman demonstrates how imitators can be kept at bay. Second-generation Walkmans are smaller and better, while containing about 50 percent fewer parts than Walkman I. Other subsequent improvements include Dolby noise reduction and a rechargeable battery. Sony keeps on innovating as well as resegmenting its market. The company has about 100 models for just about any conceivable segment. These models range from a solar-powered, waterproof Walkman for the beach and an ultralight radio-only model that attaches to a tennis player's sweatband to a tape-deck-quality unit for recording and playback.

A good defense can also be a good offense. Instead of holding the fort, the pioneer may want to attack invaders when they are neither ready nor strong. Learning that Armour-Dial wanted to introduce Pure & Natural, a mild, low-priced soap positioned at Ivory users, Procter & Gamble set out to battle. It attacked Armour-Dial's test markets, both to maintain Ivory's market and discourage Pure & Natural from expanding. In this case, Pure & Natural did well enough anyway to subsequently go national. Nonetheless, Procter & Gamble's offensive strategy initially caused great concern.

Lotus was so successful that its 1–2–3 spreadsheet program claimed to have an "installed base" of more than two million users and millions of "Lotus literates." Still Lotus had to face a number of competitors. Microsoft's Excel spreadsheet competed with Lotus by emphasizing Excel's graphic capabilities. Borland, however, used its lower price of $195 to generate sales of some 20,000 copies a month, an impressive figure even though the higher-priced 1–2–3, at $498, had 83,000 copies in monthly sales. In the case of Surpass, the company promised more features for the same price. To negate the threat posed by these competitors, Lotus planned to bring out an "improved" version. The new version would be marketed as a networking product which would allow a user to gain access to information stored elsewhere in computer networks—personal computers, minis, and mainframes. The plan, however, was delayed, allowing the other companies to make adjustments in their own products.

With a high-technology product, it is critical for the pioneering firm to establish its product system as the industry's standard. This is true even when it has to help competitors by licensing its product knowledge. Gillette's Trac II has licensed the twin-blade technology to its competitors.

Incompatible, competing systems serve only to confuse consumers and delay adoption. If a pioneer's product design becomes an industry standard, it can recoup its investment while enjoying the substantial advantages of experience and economies of scale. For example, the problem for CP/M started when IBM chose MS-DOS as the operating system for its PCs. Not long after, Microsoft's DOS became the industry standard, threatening the existence of CP/M. Likewise, Sony learned a bitter lesson from its unsuccessful attempt to go it alone with its Beta system. That decision allowed the VHS system of Victor Co. of Japan to woo other manufacturers and become the standard of video cassette recorders. Battered but wiser, Sony waited patiently for the consensus standard for the 8-mm camcorder (a camera and tape recorder in one unit) to develop. The industry finally adopted the standard guidelines in 1983, and Sony now has an agreement with 127 manufacturers on standards for this product.

IBM had a number of problems in getting its OS/2 system to replace MS/DOS. Potential buyers were hesitant to make a switch due to the OS/2 system's higher prices. Moreover, they were familiar with PCs and would have to get accustomed to a new kind of floppy disk and a new way of inserting printed-circuit cards in order to add new accessories.

To make matters worse, 80 percent of computer users were happy with PCs and the only changes desired were for PCs to be smaller, faster, and quieter. The old standard has thus held on, aided by other computer makers' strategies to prolong the life cycle of PCs. As explained earlier, it was thus a good strategic move for IBM to license its OS/2 technology to its competitors in order to gain market acceptance.

"IT CAN GET BETTER, NOT OLDER"—AN EXPANSION STRATEGY

PLC suggests that a product is most profitable when it is growing and that it becomes less profitable when it is declining. This finding suggests that the marketer should attempt to set his strategies to keep sales growing instead of letting sales decline. The product does not have to decline; it can become better and not obviously older. Many older persons stay attractive as they age when they take care of themselves instead of letting themselves go into decline. Similarly, products should be updated to stay attractive. Tide, as commented in 1977 by Procter & Gamble's chief executive officer, has been significantly modified 55 times in its 19 years.

After the crash of the video game market, Nintendo was able to revive the market by updating its product line. Unlike the original shoot-'em-up games, the new games have more recreational and educational value. These games provide good graphics at affordable prices. Nintendo thus was largely responsible for creating a new wave, although smaller than the first wave, of video game popularity.

Barbie is another product that does not seem to get any older. Barbie has changed, however. In 1985, after 25 years of partying and dating, she has matured to become a career-minded woman. The working woman version of the Barbie doll comes with such accessories as a business suit, a briefcase, a computer terminal, and a gold credit card. These changes were made to keep up with the trend of more working women, a common sight to little girls.

A product should be updated to keep up with changing lifestyles and culture. Alternative greeting cards are an example of how companies can respond to consumers' changing lifestyles. These cards are not sugarcoated like conventional cards. Recognizing baby boomers' tastes, these alternative cards use humor, sarcasm, outrageousness, and distinctive graphics. From 200 companies having 5 percent of the card market in 1983, the figures in 1985 were some 500 companies marketing alternative cards with a 15 percent market share.

In the same vein, no firm should abandon its mature products just because they have been around for a while. The time a product has been in the market is irrelevant to its worth. Many products appear to remain in the maturity stage forever without slipping over into the decline stage. Liquors and automobiles are prime examples.

Indeed, for many companies, their mature, proven products may be their major assets. Good marketers distinguish between products that are both old and declining and those that, although seemingly old, can perhaps be rejuvenated by proper support, more intensive promotion, and better positioning. As long as mature products are not likely to be replaced by new technologies within the near future, the company should try to make these products work even harder, thereby extending the mature portion of their cycle indefinitely.

Demand for home entertainment products is not stagnant because these products keep getting better and more versatile. A new generation of TV sets now provides such features as cable-ready capability, stereo sound, remote control, PIP (picture in picture), digital tuning, and so on. It will not be long before TV set manufacturers replace the obsolete PAL 525-line system with new technology capable of providing far superior picture clarity. The demand will then probably explode, and manufacturers will ride the PLC high again.

Current Users

Adapted from the idea of Levitt, there are three basic strategies which can keep products growing.[3] These strategies are aimed at: (1) current users, (2) new users, and (3) new market.

With regard to current users, the strategies involve encouraging consumers to use the product more frequently as well as in more varied ways. Hallmark Cards, for example, has created video greeting cards in addition to the creation and promotion of Grandfather's Day to stimulate card purchases. B.F. Trappey & Sons has a pamphlet of recipes with Tabasco sauce as one of the ingredients. Many food companies have also used the same approach, all with the idea of getting their products to be used more often and in more ways than one. In the case of Heinz, it suggests that housewives use its vinegar to clean their coffee machines. Not satisfied with just this varied usage, Heinz stresses that the vinegar should be used full-strength with no dilution.

Blamed for heart diseases, egg consumption has declined from 403 eggs per capita in 1945 to 251 in 1986. Fortunately for the egg industry, with the help of scientific information consumer perceptions are gradually changing for the better. Still, it is important for egg producers to educate the public about the egg's benefits. Eggs are an excellent source of high-quality protein, iron, vitamin A, vitamin B1, riboflavin, and other vitamins and minerals. The egg's other advantages are low calories and low cost. Moreover, egg producers should point out the versatility of their product. The egg is versatile because: (1) it can be fixed for breakfast, brunch, lunch, light supper, dinner, and snacks or appetizers, (2) it can be fried, poached, baked, scrambled, or cooked in the shell, (3) it can leaven souffles or thicken sauces and custards, (4) it can be used to bind ingredients such as meat loaf, coat foods for frying, and emulsify and clarify sauces. The "incredible, edible egg" campaign is the message in the right direction.

Coke's strategy of trying to get current users to drink more Coke involves promoting it as a morning drink. During the past four decades, the drinking trend has been to move away from hot, arid drinks toward colder, sweeter drinks. Having a soft drink in the morning is what Americans in the South have done for years. Coke thus wants to show that the drink is suitable for breakfast and with donuts. Eventually, the goal is to market Coke as "an any-time-of-day drink."

Of course, it is possible to combine both frequent-usage and varied-usage strategies together within the usage of the product. The orange growers have tried to increase consumption of oranges by using the theme "orange juice is not just for breakfast anymore." Their commercials showed people drinking orange juice with lunch and dinner, after a tennis match, and at other social occasions. The ultimate purpose of the message is to get people to have more frequent, more varied, usage.

New Users

A product will continue growing as long as it can attract new users. It is possible to find new users by creating new product forms for the existing product class. Poultry producers seem to have outdone their other fresh meat competitors in terms of new product forms. Perdue has added value to its fresh products by marketing the poultry's pre-cooked, prepounded, and breaded versions. In fact, some 55 percent of Tyson Foods's products are further processed. They are deboned, cooked, and offered to the market in dozens of forms. In addition, Tyson also markets a line of upscale, low-calorie frozen entrees.

More varied usage through new product forms has been used successfully by brand-name drug makers to fight generics. Several companies have reformulated their drugs for new users. The drugs have been repackaged for easier use. Abbott, for instance, broadened the market base of its popular Erythromycin antibiotic by introducing tablets and injectables in a variety of dosage forms.

The strategies to keep products growing through finding new users are not limited to only durable or expensive products. The initial popularity of Levi's 501 button-fly, shrink-to-fit jeans among gay men led to more success later in the mass market. This very old product was then modified for women.

Campbell Soup has tried to find new users by repositioning some of its staple products. The company has converted all Swanson brand containers from aluminum to paper in order to cash in on the expanding use of microwave ovens, resulting in a 50 percent increase in sales.

New Market

To create a new market while extending the life cycle of a product, it is a good idea to make a new product based on the basic materials or technology of the existing product. Texas Instruments's Speak and Spell is an extension of its technical knowledge derived from producing other educational products. Later this technical process was extended to Magic Wand Speaking Reader. With this new product, preschool children can teach themselves to read by sliding a hand-held wand across bar-code strips printed under words to decipher vocal instructions.

In the case of VLI Corp., its success with Today sponge as a birth control device led it to investigate using sponges in other areas. One promising area is to use sponges to administer drugs for vaginitis and sexually transmitted diseases, since many competing delivery methods are messy aesthetically and therapeutically.

Although the success of compact discs has already been assured, the product will gain even more success with new variations and added features. One product variation is accomplished by squeezing visuals onto the compact disc's unused space, making it possible to have compact discs with graphics that can show lyrics, artist's biography, and special effects on the TV screen. The product can further expand sound and video capability with such variations as CD-I (compact disc interactive) and DV-I (digital video interactive). In addition, the compact disc can also serve as a new method of storing and retrieving data. It has the capability of storing 300,000 pages of text.

DuPont has produced at least 2.4 billion pounds of Teflon, and this figure does not even include the SilverStone and SilverStone Supra. DuPont has planned to have three price points for the various segments. Thus it has reintroduced Teflon 2 for low-end cookwear in order to recapture the low-end market which can be traded up later. Moreover, Teflon is also made available in a spray can to coat neckties which then repel food stains and to coat light switches against dirty fingers. As a result, Teflon is in a new market with Scotchgard as its competitor.

New Packaging

One way of stimulating demand in a mature market is through new packaging. Heinz, for example, offers the squeeze bottle for its ketchup. To gain market share, Quaker State told its customers to "say good-bye to America's favorite can of motor oil." The message had to do with the company being the first to introduce a new container with a built-in pouring funnel that can be recapped.

To make milk more versatile for consumption, the milk industry has introduced a new container—aseptically packaged milk which can stay fresh for three months without refrigeration. Furthermore, the Sip Ups brand is a low fat milk in a variety of flavors such as vanilla, chocolate, and fruit punch. Milk also has been repositioned as an alternative to soft drinks. The aseptically packaged milk is thus stored in the nonrefrigerated section with fruit drinks.

New Product Design

From time to time, a product may have to be redesigned to conform to consumers' tastes. Samsonite redesigned its garment bag because of customer complaints. The new bag has pockets for shoes and small items, a feature deemed important by travelers. Pyrex, likewise, has finally changed the 50-year-old design of its measuring cup. Based on users' opinions, the new design has a more comfortable handle. Also the new cups can be stacked. The old ones had a stacking problem because of the looped-around handles. Furthermore, the new cup is deeper as a result of the complaint of liquid boiling over in the old, shallow cup when used in microwave ovens.

Demand can also be stimulated with more versatile versions of products. The appliance industry has been buoyed by a new generation of machines with electronic touch-pad controls and flashing diagnostic readouts to minimize repairmen's visits. General Electric, for example, has a dishwasher with a programmable timer. The sales of its refrigerators with electronic controls have far exceeded projections. In the future, a dishwasher can be designed to know how long to run based on the amount of soil on dishes. An oven can have an optical reader to read the frozen food's bar code for cooking instructions.

Line and Brand Extensions

To keep sales growing, a company should consider either line extensions or brand extensions or both. Line extension is a strategy to attract competitors' customers or to convince current customers to use the line more often. To give customers reasons to use the line more, the product line should be extended to include new variations (e.g., sizes, colors, flavors, scents, etc.). The line extension strategy can also be used to attract new segments or markets (i.e., current nonusers of the product).

Brand extension is the strategy to extend a brand, usually a popular one, by putting the name on new products. Let's consider Champion's brand extensions. The spark plug market is a shrinking one. With smaller engines comes use of fewer plugs. Also modern engines make it unnecessary to have frequent tune-ups. This fact has not been overlooked by the Champion Spark Plug Co. To fight its way out of this unfavorable situation, the company began to use its valuable trademark (i.e., the Champion name) on a score of new products, including air filters, ignition cables, car batteries, and fuel additives.

Other than the fact that the same brand name is used on new products, brand extension is a special kind of line extension. It may be difficult to tell the two strategies apart. Just like line extension, brand extension can be used to take advantage of either existing or new markets. Procter & Gamble, for example, has created several new detergents bearing the Tide name. By 1986, there were five Tide variations ranging from the liquid form to the unscented version and that which has fabric softener and whitener. The Jell–O name, in contrast, was put on a new product category altogether in 1984—Jell–O Pudding Pops, a frozen dessert on a stick made from Jell–O pudding. Whereas the Tide example is more of an example of utilizing an existing market, the Jell–O example is the case of a new market.

Product Positioning and Repositioning

Product positioning can be used to create or revive demand. Colgate-Palmolive, for example, has positioned its Dentagard brand as a plaque-fighting toothpaste. The brand, however, is more of a marketing innovation than a technological one since Dentagard is essentially the same toothpaste long sold by the company. The fact is that plaque is removed by brushing—not by toothpaste (or chemical ingredient).

When a product fails to perform as expected, it may need repositioning. Chelsea was first positioned as a "not-so-soft drink." When the message concerning its alcohol attribute created an uproar, Chelsea was repositioned as a "natural alternative." The repositioning, however, did not work, and the product was soon withdrawn from the market.

When the market matures, product repositioning may also be necessary. The aim is to capture new consumers. Even a successful product like Alka Seltzer was repositioned. After 52 years as a headache and upset-stomach remedy for overindulgence, Alka Seltzer was promoted as a remedy for the pressures that come with overachievement or upward mobility. The company addressed a "junior executive who vowed to be vice president by the end of the fiscal year" and mentioned in the advertisement that Alka Seltzer is "for those symptoms of stress that come with success."

Sometimes the repositioning is necessitated by new scientific evidence which adversely affects demand. Coppertone tanning lotion was well known around the world for its small mutt pulling at the bathing briefs of a small girl. Unfortunately, this message does not appeal to the health-oriented public any longer because of the link between the sun and skin cancer. The company thus has to come up with a new promotional message: the product is now, instead of for tanning, for "suncare" to help prevent premature aging, wrinkling, and skin cancer.

Any repositioning must be carefully considered so as not to offend the product's core users. Gatorade, initially promoted as a rehydrating beverage for athletes, gained moderate success through this narrow positioning. Quaker Oats bought Gatorade in 1983. Thinking that Gatorade was poorly positioned in the past, the company repositioned the product as the ultimate thirst quencher for physical-activity enthusiasts ("anyone who sweats"). What used to be a narrow but solid positioning now became broad positioning, in the process alienating core users who could not relate to amateurs. The company quickly retreated to the narrow positioning, portraying users as accomplished but not professional athletes. Although narrow positioning in terms of users and user occasions provides a limited growth opportunity, it does not alienate loyal users. Learning from the mistake, Quaker Oats now does not want to stray too far from the original positioning and attempts to target similar markets such as runners and basketball players. The company still wants to reach other broader markets more carefully by appealing to Hispanics and mothers with active children. Moreover, the company tries to market Gatorade as a year-round, not seasonal, drink. It also offers new product forms such as the 16 oz. container, four-pack, lemonade flavor, and powder form.

"MILKING CASH COWS"—A TRANSITION STRATEGY

Where products are indeed mature, the marketer must look for replacements for contemporary "stars." "Milking cash cows" means using the resources generated by mature products to support the needs of new and growing alternates. Salt, for instance, is Morton's largest and most profitable product. But salt is now at best a mature business, depending on whether the current annual decline in its consumption is temporary or permanent. The desire for low-sodium diets seems to be more than just a fad and is swiftly spreading. To cope with this threat, Morton plans to use salt as a cash cow to finance its purchases of businesses in the chemicals or household-products industries.

Likewise, Xerox, faced with the threat of lower-cost, lower-priced Japanese copiers, has been shifting from its traditional product lines. Its financial services, such as insurance, leasing, mutual funds, and investment banking, now account for half of Xerox's profits. These businesses provide greater profit margins and are expected to grow significantly.

The "milking" strategy must be used carefully. In many cases, a firm's image and reputation are strongly associated with its mature products. It is risky to divert resources too quickly from these simply to underwrite the still-uncertain future of new products the company may want to introduce. Greyhound, for example, is well known for its bus services— the business it has abandoned in favor of other ventures. Now the company is even in the process of questioning what seems to have been at one time unthinkable of Greyhound: Should it drop the highly recognized corporate name?

Using "cash cows" to buy time is only a short-run strategy. Thus, this course of action should supplement other long-term strategies. Uniroyal, although wanting to reduce its reliance on the tire business, still views tires as being important to its long-term goal. Tires have high returns which can help the company make the shift toward more non-tire businesses, with chemicals currently being given top priority in the company's annual capital budget plan.

"TRACKING NEW TECHNOLOGIES"—A STRATEGY FOR THE FUTURE

With improvement in technology, a company should consider using it in improving its existing product or in creating new products. Blade companies have worked on new shaving methods. Bic test marketed a shaver with a metal bar parallel to the blade, helping prop the skin at a better shaving angle. Schick used blades coated with polyethyline oxide that, upon contact with water, forms a lubricating strip. Gillette is working on a multi-flexible razor, a new system which cuts hair at a perpendicular angle. It can move sideways in addition to pivoting up and down, enabling the razor head to conform to facial contours.

The advance of technology eventually affects every person and product. A bank that ignores electronic banking may not be around in the future. Paper companies and newspaper executives should be aware that new electronic technologies insure that their product is no longer the only means of storing, displaying, and retrieving information.

Executives in many industries often assume that a technological change in one industry will not affect their industry and that their products will last forever. Some resist technological change because they want to play it safe with the existing technology or because they underestimate or misunderstand technology's potential.

Technological improvement in any field is eventually limited by the laws of nature and the S-curve, which implies that redirection is needed when existing products become mature. The best of manual typewriters are no match for electric typewriters, which in turn are no threat to electronic typewriters. None of them can beat word processors, which are still inferior to personal computers. The abacus was swallowed by the slide rule. Both slide rules and mechanical adding machines fell prey to the more technologically advanced electronic calculators. It would thus be foolish for anyone to try to design a more sophisticated slide rule or an advanced mechanical adding machine to compete with electronic calculators. It is also folly to believe that the best calculator can be improved technologically to a level competitive with PCs. Makers of computers have so far been able to overcome hurdles every time it seemed that the technological limit was about to be reached. Although there seems to be no viable alternative to computers within the foreseeable future, "wise" computer firms must keep an eye on any new competing technology.

When is it time to switch to a new technology rather than continue with an existing one? Several key indicators show when an existing technology (its S-curve) is approaching its limits.[4] First, there is a loss of R & D creativity and/or productivity, and R & D deadlines are missed. This problem should be expected because improvement becomes more difficult as technology limits are approached. Disharmony among the R & D staff is another warning sign, and this problem is confirmed when replacement of the staff does not result in R & D improvement. This is especially troublesome when there is little difference in returns despite spending substantially more (or less) than competitors on R & D over a period of years. Finally, it is time to get ready for the future when profits come from increasingly narrow market segments and when smaller competitors are gaining market share in a specialized market niche with radical approaches that, although improbable, may possibly work.

The above indicators should alert management to become aware that a product is approaching the end of its useful life. The awareness and preparation should help management to ride the PLC more smoothly. A failure to recognize these critical warning signs can make a large company become much smaller in a hurry.

PRODUCT DELETION STRATEGIES

A company should conduct a periodic and systematic evaluation of its product mix to determine the worthiness of each product within the mix. A product that no longer serves a useful purpose should be deleted from the mix. Yet according to one study, 60 percent of the responding firms did not have product-elimination programs. The reasons offered for this oversight include: desire to offer full product line, product cost, possible customer alienation, vested interests, disruption of routine, and lack of information.

Deletion Rules

When should a product be deleted? There are guidelines which can be used to decide the fate of a product. First, a company should ask whether the product in question is still consistent with the company's mission or future direction. Beatrice, for example, has decided to focus on synergy and has eliminated some 50 businesses including steel tubing and agricultural gear. Nabisco Brands, likewise, decided to concentrate on its strengths in packaged foods and snacks. As a result, those businesses which did not fit this strategy were sold off, and they included Aqua Velva, Geritol, Vivarin, Julius Wile Sons (liquor and wine importer), coffee, fructose sweetener, and Freezer Queen Foods.

Another decision rule requires a company to compare all existing and potential products in terms of opportunities. Given the demand on management time and a company's limited resources, a good old product may have to give way to a newer, more promising product. A company may thus want to abandon a successful old-timer so that resources can be released for products with better opportunities.

Libby, McNeill & Libby, for instance, decided to sell its well known canned fruit and vegetable line because it wanted to move away from commodities and to focus on high-tech value-added products. It thus preferred to concentrate on such products as Daybreak breakfast drink mix (the only one at the time made with real orange juice) and the Libby Lite low-calorie canned fruit line, both of which offer higher prices and profits.

Another method of determining whether it is time to delete a product is to consider the profit or return on investment of each product. Those products which offer marginal or no contribution should be dropped or divested. It was surprising to find that Maytag had held on to its wringer washing machines for years without profit. The sales of these hand-operated units peaked in 1948 and have since steadily declined to account for less than one percent of the U.S. washing machine market. Given the high price of the manual machines (around $500 a unit) and the superiority of automatic washers, there was no justification for Maytag to continue making just a few dozen of these machines each day.

Texas Instruments likewise decided to discard such low-margin products as watches, the magnetic bubble memory, liquid crystal and plasma panel displays, appliance electronics, and some semiconductor devices. Sunbeam similarly rid itself of such marginally profitable products as coffee makers, toaster ovens, deep-fat fryers, and electric knives.

Market share can also serve as a deletion rule. Market share and profit are often highly related. As the market share of a product declines, usually so does profit. The declines of the market share and profit are often a sign of fading demand and increasing competition.

A product, however, should not be hastily dropped. Management must determine whether the decline in market share is due to the maturity (or obsolescence) of the product or a lack of marketing support. A further critical consideration is whether a product can be rejuvenated. Right Guard, once a star performer with profits of some $500 million for Gillette over a two-decade period, saw its market share of 25 percent drop to just 8 percent. Gillette, instead of letting the product die, decided to give it another chance. Supported with coordinated plans which included a new container design and the company's most expensive advertising campaign, sales started to climb again and performed even better than projected.

Deletion Methods

Once a decision to drop a product is reached, other decisions are necessary. Orderly deletion is a must, and strategies must be devised to minimize losses and retain customer good will. In many cases, a company cannot just pack up and leave.

Product withdrawal can be either *complete* or *partial*. A company has the option of withdrawing the total product line from the market altogether. Texas Instruments, for instance, withdrew its complete home computer line due to unsatisfactory performance. Or the company may elect partial withdrawal (i.e., product line simplification). Mennen, in its effort to get rid of marginal products, simplified its Balm Barr line of cocoa-based women's skin care products by reducing the dozen varieties it had in its product line and ended up with just four items.

Product withdrawal can also be either *immediate* or *gradual*. For a product which is clearly unsuitable because of safety reasons or large losses, it may be better to cut the losses short and leave the market right away. For those with marginal profits but with some existing demand and profit contribution, it is probably wise to make the withdrawal more gradual. For the purpose of gradual deletion, the strategies may involve product line simplification and/or price increase. Hiram Walker used the latter strategy to price its declining brands (e.g., Imperial blended whisky) out of existence.

Any decision concerning product deletion should be made with dealers and consumers in mind. Although a company can stop producing a product, it cannot ignore its obligations related to customer service. Parts and repair facilities are required until the product is no longer in use. When RCA withdrew from the videodisc market, it was compelled to continue pressing discs for the owners of its videodisc players for

three additional years. This was necessary because of the need to maintain good will on the one hand. On the other hand, with some 500,000
players in the market, it was important to avoid potential lawsuits,
legitimate or not, which could easily be brought by disgruntled customers who felt that their costly purchases and investments were be-
trayed.

Somewhat related to the point made above, dealers should not be left
with unwanted inventories which are rapidly declining in value. A manufacturer must keep on advertising its withdrawn product in order to
move the inventory for itself as well as for its dealers. Incentives in terms
of price reduction will have to be offered to clear out inventories quickly.
When IBM and Texas Instruments dropped their home computer systems, both continued to advertise the products while slashing prices.
Such action is necessary due to economic, legal, and social reasons. If
dealers are abandoned, a manufacturer may lose their loyalty and future
support. On the next occasion the company decides to get back into the
market, the distribution channel which it destroyed will not be available
for the new marketing effort.

As evidenced by its 65 percent market share of the education market,
there is no question that the Apple II computer has forever changed the
way that people work and learn. Just as undeniable is the fact that the
aging Apple II is near the end of its PLC. It is now a wise move for
Apple not to commit too much of its resources to the Apple II line.
Although denying it, Apple has prepared for the day when the Apple
II will be dropped and replaced by the technologically superior and more
expensive Macintosh computer. Yet the Apple II line still offers the
company a great deal of profit, contributing nearly $700 million or one-
third of the company's total revenue. This contribution makes it desirable
to "milk" the Apple II line during the coming transition. Toward this
goal, the company has added the IIgs line which is compatible with the
Apple II line of software while offering more built-in power (memory)
and superior sound and graphics. Users of the IIgs can also connect the
IIgs to stereo speakers and an analog color monitor for a wider range
of colors. It thus appears that the IIgs line was primarily designed to
extend Apple II's market viability for a few more years.

COMPANY/MANAGEMENT LIFE CYCLE

A relatively new marketing idea based on PLC suggests that it is
desirable to match managerial style with a product life cycle stage. This
hypothesis, though thought-provoking, has not been conclusively
proved or widely accepted. But this hypothesis appears to have merit
and deserves further investigation.

The basic and conventional principles of management indicate that a good manager will always perform satisfactorily—regardless of time, product, industry, and company. This is the regimen desired and practiced by most firms. Some theorists, however, insist that different kinds of managers are needed for the different stages of a company and/or its product. In the early stage, an entrepreneurial type of manager is needed because his strong points are risk-taking, energetic drive, and the willingness to accept innovation. Texas Instruments made a mistake by replacing a brilliant scientist who was not a strong manager for its new product because of his research orientation. But it was only after an interval of time and some reflection that the company realized that this was exactly the type of individual needed at that stage. After committing several other similar mistakes, Texas Instruments eventually recognized the problem and went on to become successful in the metal oxide semiconductor technology. The lesson learned by the company was: "As a product moves through different phases of its life cycle, different kinds of management skills become dominant."[5]

As the product grows and matures, the entrepreneurial manager soon loses favor as the right kind of person for the next stage. A successful entrepreneur in the first stage is often flamboyant, autocratic, strong willed, high-strung, energetic, fast talking, and eager to maintain the company in an informal, flexible, entrepreneurial way. Nonetheless, these characteristics are not required nor even desirable in this next stage. This is the time for the kind of manager who can cut costs, increase productivity, and provide stable sales and profits; a risk taker would only aggravate the situation because his managerial style inevitably creates wide swings in profit, sales, and performance. The problem can be illustrated by most founders' inability to let go of the companies they have started. Edwin Land and Hugh Hefner have long ceased to be positive assets for their enterprises (Polaroid and Playboy, respectively). Other entrepreneurs, however, have recognized the problem and been able to transfer power from themselves to others more smoothly.

Trammel Crow, for example, the nation's largest real estate developer, reduced his stock holdings to 33 percent and sold most of his stock to his executives to reduce his domination. An Wang, aware of his company's growth, has started to transfer the major responsibilities he has held to a managing committee and his son.

If the company life cycle hypothesis is valid, an appropriate advertisement for managerial personnel might read, "Help Wanted: Growers, Defenders, and Undertakers." It is wise to match managerial talent to the different stages of the company and its product in order to avoid disharmony and to increase performance.

As illustrated in the case of Best Western International, its chief executive officer brought the chain from 800 to 2,597 units in the early 1980s and wanted to continue adding units, while the owners wanted to curtail the company's growth. The chief executive officer then left for Quality Inns, where there was no system involving democratic membership voting rules and the company still saw itself in the early stages of life cycle.[6] General Electric is an example of a company that has perhaps gone farther than others in adopting the concept of company/ product life cycle. Based on the concept of the product life cycle, General Electric defines its products as "grow," "defend," and "harvest." These categories result in managers being classified as growers, caretakers, and undertakers in order to match a certain kind of manager with the product's status.

In conclusion, the company life cycle concept offers several strategic implications which should be investigated further. Studies should be conducted to answer whether a special manager with special skills for a particular stage of the company's life cycle can perform significantly better than the versatile, general, Jack-of-all-trades type manager. One thing is certain, however: A good manager must recognize the life cycle stages of his products, and he must ascertain whether his skills and personal characteristics will be an asset or a hindrance under the circumstances in which the company finds itself.

CONCLUSION

PLC and marketing strategies are compatible partners, not the odd couple. In addition to the general rules for adjusting the marketing mix, the product life cycle also suggests several propositions that would be of help in the marketplace. These include: (1) it is often preferable to be an imitator rather than a pioneer, (2) a pioneer should anticipate and devise strategies in advance to prevent or slow down imitation, (3) a product must be sustained in order to keep it growing and not declining, (4) the marketer should plan the necessary transition steps to change course smoothly from an older product to a younger one, and (5) it is necessary to be alert for new technological trends rather than to offer resistance to them.

Theory is a means to an end, and the value of a particular theory must ultimately rest on its ability to offer pragmatic insights for marketers to improve their performance. PLC scores well on this criterion. The PLC concept does make significant contribution in terms of the "control" function.

PLC and the marketing mix are both interactive and interdependent. A change in one, regardless of whether it is a cause or effect, will significantly affect the other. This association is analogous to the relationship between a man's physical health based on his age and his physical exercise. A good exercise program should keep him physically fit for his age, which in turn can lengthen his life. Yet his health is still greatly affected by his age (i.e., life cycle) independent of how much exercise he does. Based on the same rationale, a brilliant and intensive marketing campaign is unlikely to bring back to life such obsolete products as manual typewriters, wringer washing machines, vacuum-tube TVs, or mechanical cash registers.

PLC also provides a basis for product analysis. Notwithstanding, the concept should not be taken on blind faith and used as a substitute for logical judgment. In any case, PLC is a valuable tool that suggests a proper course of action to lessen the impact of competitive changes. In the search for a differential advantage, it provides normative implications for decision making. Due to its strategic implications, PLC is too valuable a business tool to relegate to textbooks. It belongs in the corporate board room, on center stage.

NOTES

1. These strategies are based on Sak Onkvisit and John J. Shaw, "Competition and Product Management: Can the Product Life Cycle Help?" *Business Horizons* 29 (July/August 1986): 51–62.

2. "Hiram Walker: A Move into Rum Fills a Major Product Gap," *Business Week*, 24 April 1978, pp. 92–93.

3. Theodore Levitt, "Exploit the Product Life Cycle," *Harvard Business Review* 43 (November-December 1965): 81–94.

4. Richard N. Foster, "A Call for Vision in Managing Technology," *Business Week*, 24 May 1984, pp. 24–33.

5. "Wanted: A Manager to Fit Each Strategy," *Business Week*, 25 February 1980, pp. 166ff.

6. "Matching Manager to a Company's Life Cycle," *Business Week*, 23 February 1981, pp. 62ff.

PART IV

INTERNATIONAL DIMENSION

7

International Product Life Cycle

PRODUCT LIFE CYCLE—DOMESTIC AND INTERNATIONAL

With some exceptions as noted earlier in other chapters, a successful product usually passes through a series of stages of the life cycle. Assuming no cultural barriers, the phenomenon should repeat itself again in markets abroad each time a product is introduced in a new country. Of course, this does not mean that the product will go through these stages in all countries at exactly the same time or at the same pace. What it means is that product life cycle, with differences in timing and time intervals, is frequently a universal phenomenon.

In addition to its local or domestic life cycle within a particular country, a successful product may also possess another distinct cycle based on multinational sales behavior. This overseas cycle, known as the international product life cycle (IPLC), is highly useful in explaining and predicting competitive trends—at home and abroad. As such, the international product life cycle has implications for the innovating firm, especially if it plans to expand overseas. Even if there is no interest in overseas markets, a firm should still find the IPLC very relevant, especially where threats from overseas competition may exist.

The rationale for the study of IPLC is the same as that for the study of the domestic PLC: competitive changes. As a product moves through the various stages of its international life cycle, the local as well as the international competitive environment will change accordingly. The dynamic nature of markets at home and abroad will make it necessary to adjust marketing strategy in response to changing market conditions. All of the four Ps in marketing mix will be affected by such changes.

IPLC THEORY

The IPLC describes how a new product, based on a new technology or production process, is diffused on an international scale. The cycle begins with a firm, usually in an advanced nation, developing and introducing a new product which offers the market a significant benefit. Once the local market becomes relatively well developed or saturated, the product is exported—first to other advanced countries and later to less developed countries (LDCs). Initially, these countries lag in terms of the technological expertise required to produce the product. But before long, other advanced countries learn how to manufacture the product in question, and LDCs soon follow suit. Such countries, upon acquiring the technology, not only produce the product for their own domestic consumption but will also attempt to market the surplus back to the initiating country.

There are several reasons why advanced nations are likely to be the place for innovation introduction and/or the initial entry point for overseas markets. From a supply standpoint, firms in advanced nations have abundant capital, a factor of production which is needed to develop, test, and market a new product. In addition, these firms have technological know-how and are more likely to carry out basic research—something that LDCs have difficulty in matching due to other pressing and immediate needs coupled with limited resources. These reasons force (or encourage) LDCs to instead emphasize applied research. The highly developed mass production and market systems in advanced countries also make it easier to begin the innovation there. From the customer point of view, customers in advanced countries favor new products which can improve their standard of living. In addition, these customers are relatively affluent, with adequate disposable/discretionary incomes which can be used to purchase new products despite initial high price.

For ease of discussion, the assumption will be made that a U.S. company is the one which introduces a new product and that the innovation is first introduced in the United States. This assumption is not unreasonable since the United States does a great deal of basic research and American consumers' needs are practically insatiable. According to one study, U.S. firms were responsible for 63.8 percent of 500 significant innovations.[1] However, it should be noted that in 1987, Japanese firms obtained more U.S. patents than their American counterparts.

Exhibit 7.1 provides a brief and concise look at the various stages of the IPLC as well as the changing competitive conditions as they occur within the innovating country. Exhibit 7.2 provides a graphic illustration of the competitive changes experienced by the various countries involved.[2] There are actually three IPLC curves for the same product, one for each country or group of countries that is involved. It should be noted that the direction of each curve changes as the innovation moves through time. Time is relative in the sense that the time periods for all stages are neither fixed nor equal. The type of product and competitive action that takes place will determine the length of time needed for the change and for each curve to complete its cycle.

Each IPLC curve reveals the situation regarding a country's net export (or import) volume. The horizontal line, as a benchmark, is the point at which there is no net export or net import (i.e., the point where export equals import). The export level of a country is indicated by how far its IPLC curve moves above the horizontal line (i.e., time axis), while the extent that the curve is below the line shows the import level.

As shown in Exhibits 7.1 and 7.2, IPLC has four distinct stages. For our purpose, the discussion will begin with stage one, since it is this period when export begins to take place and the IPLC is actually initiated.

Stage 1: Overseas Innovation

Stage 1 begins the IPLC. This stage may be called the "international pioneering" or "international entry" stage, since an innovating firm, after largely satisfying local demand, seeks to capitalize on its technological edge by looking for marketing opportunities abroad. It is practical in the first move overseas to involve other advanced nations (Western

Exhibit 7.1
IPLC Stages and Characteristics (for the Initiating Country)

Stage	Import/Export	Target Market	Competitors	Production Costs
0) local innovation	none	USA	few: local firms	initially high
1) overseas innovation	increasing export	USA & advanced nations	few: local firms	decline due to economies of scale
2) maturity	stable export	advanced nations & LDCs	advanced nations	stable
3) worldwide imitation	declining export	LDCs	advanced nations	increase due to lower economies of scale
4) reversal	increasing import	USA	advanced nations & LDCs	increase due to comparative disadvantage

Source: Sak Onkvisit and John J. Shaw, "An Examination of the International Product
    Life Cycle and Its Application Within Marketing," *Columbia Journal of World
    Business* 18 (Fall 1983): 74.

European countries, Canada, Australia, New Zealand, and Japan). These
advanced countries are a wise choice because consumers there are similar
to their U.S. counterparts in terms of taste and income. The English-
speaking countries (the United Kingdom, Canada, and Australia) are
especially attractive. As the product gains wider acceptance in other
advanced countries, the export volume of the United States will correspondingly increase.

Stage 2: Maturity

Similar to the maturity stage of the regular PLC, a major characteristic
of the second stage of the IPLC is "stability." The sales/export volume
of the initiating firm remains relatively stable throughout this stage.
Unlike the regular PLC, which has a stable number of competitors in
this stage, the IPLC experiences an increase in the number of compet-

Exhibit 7.2
IPLC Curves

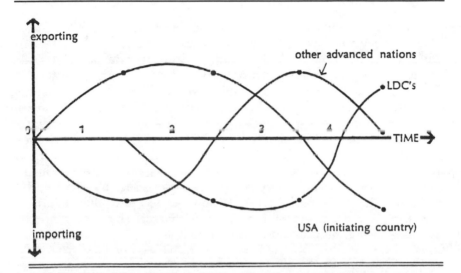

Source: Sak Onkvisit and John J. Shaw, "An Examination of the International Product
Life Cycle and Its Application Within Marketing," *Columbia Journal of World
Business* 18 (Fall 1983): 74.

itors. The demand in advanced nations has by now been well cultivated, but the increase in demand there is not converted into a corresponding increase in the innovator's export volume. This is the case because firms in these advanced nations, recognizing the market potential, attempt to narrow the technological gap and begin to produce the product. Encouraged by government assistance and perhaps subsidies for infant industries, these firms are able to establish production facilities through their countries' protective measures. Fortunately, any loss of sales to the U.S. innovator in such markets is offset by the opening of new markets, with LDCs now being the next adopter group showing interest in importing the product. In this way, the innovator's export volume, although not increasing, continues to be healthy.

Stage 3: Worldwide Imitation

In this stage, the export situation deteriorates for the United States. There are several reasons why this is the case. The demand in LDCs for the product has now peaked, resulting in no new demand. To make matters worse, other advanced nations, not only being self-sufficient, export their excess capacity to compete with the United States in LDCs, resulting in price cutting and fierce competition. Too little demand and too much supply are the characteristics of this stage. Since all advanced nations aim their marketing efforts at LDCs, the U.S. product in these markets is partially replaced by those supplied from other advanced nations. The cost situation becomes another negative factor, because a smaller U.S. export means lower economies of scale. Near the end of this stage, the U.S. export volume continues to decline to almost nothing, and any production is mostly for the U.S. market. This is currently the situation facing the U.S. automobile industry.

Stage 4: Reversal

When it rains, it pours. This statement typifies the dilemma faced by the initiating country. Instead of being a net exporter, the innovator now has reversed roles from being a producer to being a consumer. For the United States, there is a shift from comparative advantage to one which is now replaced by comparative disadvantage. The product is no longer a novelty or a complicated item, because the product may have reached its technical limit of refinement. By this time, the main components of the product are so standardized that LDCs can easily produce simple versions of the product. It is possible to substitute factors of production in the manufacturing process for the product. The capital factor or the technology factor can be replaced by labor—a main advantage that LDCs have because of abundant labor.

IPLC IN PRACTICE

How well does the IPLC theory work in practice? There are indeed several products which conform to the behavior described by the theory. Although the United States began the black-and-white TV industry, its comparative advantage began to shift with the introduction of color television consoles. By the late 1970s, only five U.S. manufacturers remained. Not long after that, the only U.S. manufacturer of color TV sets remaining in the market was Zenith. Virtually all black-and-white TV sets are now produced abroad for consumption in the United States because Asian countries are capable of making these units at much lower cost than U.S. firms can.

Another product which has moved in the market as described by the IPLC is the microwave oven. Although invented in the United States, most microwave ovens are now manufactured by Japan and other Asian countries. In the case of this product, it took Japanese manufacturers only 15 years to replace U.S. manufacturers.

Other products that have behaved or are behaving very closely to the predicted IPLC pattern include steel, automobiles, consumer appliances, computer chips, personal computers, and tape recorders. As a matter of fact, even in the case of services such as software programming, India and the Philippines have emerged as leading software centers which adapt existing programs as well as create new software. Intel and Wang Labs, as a result, have shifted some of their programming functions to these countries.

STRATEGIC IMPLICATIONS OF IPLC

As is true in the case of the domestic PLC, a good marketing strategy can lengthen IPLC while a poor strategy can hasten the pace of the cycle. An ignorance of the implications of IPLC is one reason why many U.S. companies and industries, in spite of the threat of foreign competition, have failed to adjust their marketing strategies. Some have even taken action which has resulted in doing more harm than good.

The U.S. steel industry can serve as an example of how an industry can become a victim of international business events. After World War II, U.S. steel manufacturers held a significant edge over foreign manufacturers and by 1950 accounted for 40 percent of worldwide production. The technological superiority was clearly shown in terms of market share and export volume. As late as 1955, imports managed to account for only 1 1/4 percent of steel consumption in the United States. By 1985, however, the steel situation was nothing short of a complete reversal. U.S. steel, as a percentage of world production, fell to 11 percent, while the United States had to import steel to satisfy a quarter of its con-

Exhibit 7.3
The Decline of U.S. Steel

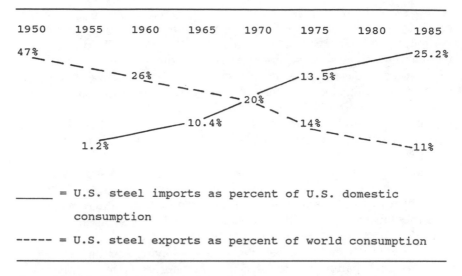

| 1950 | 1955 | 1960 | 1965 | 1970 | 1975 | 1980 | 1985 |

_____ = U.S. steel imports as percent of U.S. domestic
        consumption

\- - - - - = U.S. steel exports as percent of world consumption

Source: Lloyd R. Kenward, "The Decline of the U.S. Steel Industry," *Finance and Development* (December 1987): 30–33.

sumption needs.[3] Exhibit 7.3 shows the startling and dramatic decline of the U.S. steel industry.

What were the causes of the decline? Unfair foreign competition and environmental regulations contributed to some but not all of the decline. In addition, Japan and the European Community (EC) simply have become much more efficient, especially with the adoption of new technologies. On the other hand, the poor performance and lack of foresight of U.S. steel makers have also contributed to their failure to take appropriate action. U.S. firms have been slow and deficient in adopting such new manufacturing technologies as the electric arc approach and the process of continuous casting. Many U.S. firms chose to continue with the open-hearth technology, which is older and less efficient. Also, instead of building new and more efficient production facilities, the companies attempted to refit facilities. To make matters more complicated, steel was increasingly replaced by such lighter-weight and corrosion-resistant products as plastics, aluminum, and fiberglass.

Another problem has been the excessive wage settlements won by steel unions. Not surprisingly, the operating costs of American steel mills have become quite high. In 1964, U.S. firms' costs were 15 percent higher than those of Japanese producers. By 1972, the gap had widened to 40 percent, and such a gap could not be offset in spite of Japanese firms' costs of transportation of steel to the U.S. market.

It could also be said that many of the U.S. steel makers' problems were self-inflicted. U.S. steel firms have failed to understand the loss of technological superiority and to make timely and appropriate adjustments in strategies.

It is true that the IPLC stages recommend the marketing decisions that should be taken. But it is also important to recognize that a good marketing plan initiated by an innovating firm can favorably affect the IPLC. The following sections discuss how the marketing mix can be adjusted within each stage of the IPLC so that a competitive advantage can be achieved.

PRODUCT STRATEGY

An inventor should carefully consider the movement of the product through the different stages of the IPLC. The sequence described by the IPLC serves as a guideline for developing particular strategies. First, the initiating firm should try to dominate its own market before moving on to other advanced nations. Once these advanced nations become both customers as well as competitors, LDCs should be approached.

It should be recognized that it is a matter of time before competition emerges. Since competition is inevitable, the initiating firm should take necessary measures to delay the entry of potential competitors. One way of doing so is to obtain patents. This does not mean, however, that patents should be obtained in all markets. Due to the costs involved, a cost-benefit analysis should be performed. It may not be practical to obtain a patent in a country where certain kinds of patents are not recognized, patent enforcement is weak, or demand potential is too low.

Generally, it is desirable to obtain patents in all major industrial nations (Western Europe, Japan, Canada, and Australia) since they are likely customers as well as future competitors. The treaties that exist among nations make it possible to obtain patents simultaneously in a number of nations.

Because of weak enforcement in many LDCs, political pressure from the initiating country may be necessary to attempt to forestall competition from firms within these countries. In many cases where strong competition has been experienced by U.S. firms, this is what the United States has been doing in its attempt to stop patent infringement and counterfeiting.

Because an innovator has a competitive edge, this should not give the innovator the luxury of remaining complacent. IBM, after succeeding in becoming the standard of the personal computer industry, was surprisingly slow in reacting to imitators. Instead, it allowed Korean and Taiwanese firms as well as many other local manufacturers to easily imitate and enter the market.

It should be understood that it is just a matter of time before foreign firms can duplicate the original, basic version of the product. One countermeasure for this type of competitive behavior is to continuously upgrade a product. More innovative systems or features should be periodically added whenever possible. It is thus necessary for the innovator to continuously innovate in order to leave the competitors one step behind.

Another major factor in determining the activities within the stages of the IPLC and competitive conditions is the cost structure. When a product becomes mature—locally as well as internationally—production costs become an important factor and must be kept at a minimum. A firm which can reduce cost through automation or substitution of factors of production to its advantage can thus gain strategic advantage.

Although the IPLC appears to imply that LDCs have long-term strategic advantage through their abundant and low-cost labor, firms in advanced nations can take several courses of action that can positively affect their cost structure. Automation can reduce labor costs. This is what the United States has been implementing to fend off the Japanese threat and what the Japanese in turn are now carrying out to minimize the threat from other Asian nations with less expensive labor.

Another strategy involves using local (foreign) manufacturing. It may be desirable to set up local production facilities in a number of countries where labor is inexpensive. Atari, like many other firms making electronics products, has shifted the production of its products to the Far East.

Other advantages to be gained when overseas production is used for the purpose of entering overseas markets are minimizing transportation costs while at the same time overcoming political resistance that may stand in the way of market entry. Additionally, a company may gain low-cost production advantages which could be used to neutralize other competitors' advantages. Ingersoll-Rand, for example, has increased its reliance on manufacturing operations overseas. Its foreign plants, once responsible for 27 percent of the company's products sold abroad, are now responsible for more than 50 percent of the volume required overseas.

Local manufacturing in a low-cost country can be used to export that product to other nearby countries as well as to export the product to the United States itself. Ireland, for example, can be used for manufacturing products for consumption in the European Community (EC), while avoiding tariffs and complications of product movement within the countries of the EC.

A variation of local manufacturing is an assembly strategy that uses several production facilities located in several countries—each producing a certain component or part in order to make the most of the advantage offered by each country. These components can then be combined or assembled for distribution and consumption in a number of markets. The firm should also carefully consider the location of the assembly operation, because this would also be influenced by the required labor or technology. IBM has used this strategy for its personal computers; the various components are manufactured in a variety of countries in order to minimize costs.

There are other production strategies which may be used. One strategy may involve a shift from doing one's own production. Tool makers such as Kearney and Trecker, for example, place their own brands on Japanese-made machine tools which are sold in the United States. Another strategy involves having an agreement for the licensing and joint production of products. Houdaille Industries, a machine tool and pump manufacturer, entered into a joint production agreement with Okuma Machinery Works in order to gain Okuma's knowledge in computer-numerically controlled (CNC) lathes and other new technology. The licensing and joint production agreement provided a quick method by which Houdaille was able to acquire market-flexible manufacturing systems.

Caterpillar has stopped the practice of attempting to produce products it needs and now buys products which are made more inexpensively by others. Daewoo's lift trucks are one example of these new products. Another example is the track-type excavators made by a German firm for Caterpillar's overseas dealers. General Motors, likewise, has reduced its own production totals by purchasing foreign made automobiles and component parts.

Although the robotics industry originated in the United States in the 1960s, the United States is no longer a leader in this industry.[4] This strategic blunder came about because U.S. robots were too sophisticated and expensive for customer needs. The new leader in this industry is Japan, which was quick to follow the United States into this market. Receiving extensive government support in terms of research and development, tax incentives, and low-interest loans, Japanese firms have been able to push ahead of other competitors. Japanese robotics firms developed their own large domestic market first, and this accomplishment resulted in economies of scale. Next, the Japanese moved to enter the United States and other markets. Currently, Japan is the leader in the production of industrial robots, followed by the United States and Western Europe.

Responding to foreign competition, U.S. firms have begun to use joint ventures and license agreements with foreign firms for the manufacture of basic units. U.S. firms have developed refinements and peripherals as well as installed and adapted foreign-source equipment in their U.S. factories. American firms have also shifted their concentration more on the marketing of robotic products and less on the production of such equipment.

Just like the suggestion made by the regular (domestic) PLC, the IPLC also suggests that the initiating firm establish its product design as the worldwide standard for the industry. Nokia, a Finnish firm, has developed a system for digital cellular phones and base stations, hoping for it to become the international standard. Toward this goal, it has joined forces with France's Alcatel and West Germany's AEG. Moreover, its strategy also involves building market share in France and West Germany.

The next battleground for TV manufacturers is HDTV (high definition TV), with the European consortium fighting it out with the Japanese consortium for the right to have its own system as the industry standard. HDTV is likely to be a successful product due to its inherent advantages: a combination of the convenience of videotape with the quality of a film. It could do for the TV industry what the compact disc has done for the record industry. HDTV's potential is not restricted only to television. The technology also offers capability for a new generation of video cassette recorders with high definition as well as for industrial electronics and personal computers. Moreover, it can be useful for medical imaging, printing, movie making, and other areas of visual communications. Consumers seem so far undaunted by the projected cost of $3,500 per unit.

Sadly, the United States is not one of the contestants since the United States no longer has a consumer electronics industry. Still the U.S. market is the one which will probably decide the winning system. Not surprisingly, the battle is fierce.

Japan Broadcasting Corp. (NHK), Japan's national broadcasting company, has developed MUSE. The strength of the MUSE format is its early development and the acceptance by 35 equipment manufacturers. The Japanese initially wanted to double their own scanning lines from 525 to 1,050 and to have an operating frequency of 60. The proposed European system, however, will double the European scan from 625 to 1,250 lines, and the system will have an operating frequency of 50. The European consortium has spent over three years and $232 million on this system. As a gesture of compromise, the Japanese have agreed to increase the number of lines to 1,125.

The battle over the setting of global standards is very significant. Although the Japanese have made an early commitment, many of the consumer product firms in the United States are owned by the Europeans (e.g., GE and RCA are owned by Thomson of France). If the European firms are successful in pushing for a higher number of scanning lines and the lower frequency, it will create a big problem for the Japanese rivals because of the additional development costs, not to mention the loss of advantage of early development. To influence the U.S. standard yet to be adopted, the Japanese have contacted American politicians and provided demonstrations of their technology.

PRICING STRATEGY

With overseas markets developed and united with the initial U.S. market, the U.S. innovator can gain economies of scale, contributing more to profit because of a decline in production costs. The reduced costs, however, are not necessarily reflected in lower introductory prices abroad. The technological advantage combined with few, if any, competitors and the prestige of a new product make it prudent to command a premium price.

In many ways, the pricing strategy required for the IPLC does not differ appreciably from that suggested by the regular PLC. Initially, an innovator may want to use skimming pricing. The product should carry a high price at introduction because of product uniqueness, lack of competition due to technological edge, and cultivation of quality image.

Once the product gains acceptance and the production costs are reduced due to better economies of scale, it is only a matter of time before other firms think about making the same product. In this stage, the innovator should lower the price in order to: (1) capture the mass market, (2) be price competitive, and (3) forewarn competitors of declining margins. Caterpillar has used discount prices to discourage Komatsu from selling more of its construction machinery in the United States and other countries.

In the late stage of the cycle, low price alone cannot effectively fend off competitors. Furthermore, the low price is not practical anymore because costs are rising for the initiating firm and competitors have gained a cost advantage. If the market has been segmented, low price should only be used with the low end of the market, especially if the production of the low-priced product version shares in the fixed costs. Otherwise, a skimming price may be more appropriate, assuming that the innovator has a more sophisticated product with some unique, differentiable features, physically or psychologically. Therefore, the above-the-market price can be effective only if it is supported by meaningful product features and effective promotion campaigns.

Competitors that cannot match the initiating company's product in terms of quality or consumer perception will have to pay a penalty in the form of lower prices. Ironically, this is the strategy that Japanese firms had to follow at one time in the U.S. market. As recently as the early 1970s, Japanese products were still considered by many American consumers as being nothing more than low-quality junk. The Japanese persevered and were finally able to change consumer perceptions to their advantage. Many U.S. manufacturers, notably those in the automobile industry, not only failed to take advantage of their desirable image but also let the quality image decline to the point that American consumers now perceive Japanese products as being superior.

PROMOTION STRATEGY

Pricing and promotion strategies are highly related. How a product is promoted will affect its price perception and vice versa. As stated earlier, price competition is not always a sound strategy, especially near the end of the cycle when the initiating company's production costs are rising. A high price can be justified at the beginning of the life cycle due to the technological advantage. At the end, however, a high price must be justified less on the basis of technology and more on promotion. Therefore, it is necessary to plan for a nonprice promotional campaign from the early part of the cycle.

While a product can be standardized, its image cannot be so easily duplicated, if at all. Therefore, a product should not be permitted to become a commodity, something which is usually bought on the basis of physical grade and price. The image can be used to act as an intervening variable. A product, whenever possible, should be branded and promoted as a premium product with a high-quality image, since this is likely to offer better profit margins and protection from competitive efforts. Yet this approach still allows the company the flexibility of trading down by adding a less sophisticated version at a lower price.

The innovator has a promotional advantage since the innovator is in a position to select the proper product positioning strategy while having time to build brand awareness. Realizing that its patent would eventually expire, G. D. Searle spent great sums of money promoting the various brand names of its aspartame product. This strategy made a great deal of sense because brand awareness and knowledge were built. Once the patent expires, the company will have strategic advantage derived from the highly recognizable brand names. Any price can be easily duplicated, but it is a different matter where the high prestige of a well-known brand is concerned. Product differentiation, not price, is thus the key to keeping a product profitable by having an above-the-market price.

Pontiac once held a strong reputation because of its performance-car image in the 1960s and 1970s. Then, due to General Motors's preoccupation with production orientation, the Pontiac automobile line began to take on a similar appearance to automobiles from the other divisions of General Motors. Pontiac's image was blurred to the point of obscurity. To correct the mistake, Pontiac was repositioned as a very innovative (in terms of styling and engineering), sporty, and fun-to-drive car. Its "we build excitement" campaign was designed to proclaim Pontiac as an excitement builder. Instead of promoting Pontiac cars in general, the Pontiac division also chose to promote a specific car within each class.

PLACE (DISTRIBUTION) STRATEGY

One way of supporting a unique image and skimming pricing is by having a strong distribution network in place. This is highly practical and appropriate, since the innovating firm is in a favorable position to pick the best dealers. Dealer support is critical, and latecomers will find it difficult to secure good dealers. In addition, a newcomer may find the required network to be extremely costly, not to mention the amount of time needed to build such a distribution network. This explains why it has taken Japanese manufacturers of automobiles and electronic products a long time to gain a foothold in the United States. Ironically, Detroit's own activities have been a tremendous help to Japanese auto makers. By prohibiting its dealers from carrying its other brands or having other outlets for the same brand, General Motors forced its dealers to look for alternatives, and they found Japanese cars. Since those days, the American automobile market has never been the same.

If you cannot fight them, you may as well join them. In some cases, this is a wise strategy. Once the battle is lost in the sense that foreign products are imported and well accepted, U.S. manufacturers and middlemen may want to save whatever is left of their markets by becoming partners with their former competitors. By offering their facilities, technical help, and marketing expertise, U.S. firms can become agents and make profits from operating in a cooperative manner. Caterpillar, as one company dealing with such a situation, has finally agreed to sell non-affiliated foreign suppliers' products through its worldwide distribution network. In addition, General Motors has decided to become a marketing agent for Suzuki, Isuzu, and Daewoo.

OTHER STRATEGIES

Local marketers should also be aware of the presence of foreign invaders. In the not distant past, Japanese firms have invaded and often conquered many markets. It is thus critical for local firms to devise prior strategies in order to repel the Japanese or other foreign invaders. Some of the strategies are discussed next.

First, a local company may want to *fight fire with fire*. This means that the firm chooses to remain exactly in the same business except for the fact that it tries to increase its efficiency to match or exceed that of the competitors. This is how Inland Steel chose to contest the Japanese steel imports. It has reinvested massively to modernize and expand production facilities, upgrade quality, and reduce production costs. Instead of diversifying like other firms, Inland Steel has stayed with steel and introduced such new products as high-strength body sheet and corrosion-free steel for automobiles and farm and construction vehicles and ultra-strong steel for automobile door beams and bumper backings. Another variation of this method may involve the firm importing products or parts of products. This strategy is especially suitable in the commodity segment, where price cutting can be brutal. If American marketers cannot be cost-competitive, they will not remain in business for long.

If the local firm is not comfortable in the business that it is in and if it feels that circumstances are not going to improve, it may want to *diversify* into more promising businesses. This is the strategy used by domestic footwear makers to combat rising shoe imports. This method involves leaving a familiar market for an unfamiliar market and is not necessarily easy. Genesco chose diversification and found the transition difficult. U.S. Shoe, on the other hand, has been more successful in its diversification into specialty retailing such as Casual Corner, J. Riggins, August Max, Caren Charles, Antics, and T. H. Mandy.

Another defensive strategy recommends the use of *market segmentation*. A firm can thus concentrate on the defendable market niches. Cascade Steel, for example, was a tiny steel producer which did not share similar problems encountered by its giant brothers. It chose to concentrate on steel products at the lowest end of the profit scale—products such as narrow rods (rebar) used to reinforce poured concrete in big construction projects. By selecting a segment that the Japanese did not take an interest in, Cascade Steel has outpaced the entire industry.

Several interesting strategies have been used successfully by many domestic manufacturers as a defense against apparel imports. For those choosing to depend on the same market, several have turned to importing. Others may have chosen to acquire import-proof brands in order to use brand names as a means of neutralizing the prices of imports. For example, Interco has acquired London Fog raincoats and College Town sportswear. Such fashion-oriented or premium-priced brands can be safeguarded against cheap imports. Another variation may entail putting the name of a well-known designer on easily produced standardized garments that sell for a fraction of the price of the designer's regular line but cost more than comparable branded items. This is the direction that Puritan has followed with its Calvin Klein jeans. In the case of Evan Picone, after quitting the rapidly changing fashion market, it has adopted the strategy of concentrating on tailored women's blazers, shirts, and suits that are more timeless and serve as classical designs suitable for working women.

Sometimes a combination of strategies, rather than a single method, should be employed. Many U.S. manufacturers have cut costs and customized their products, in addition to making an effort to offer better service support after the sale. As shown in the case of Firestone, the company has retreated from the tire manufacturing business to concentrate on being a marketer of heavy truck tires. It has also spent heavily diversifying into healthier sales-and-service-oriented businesses such as automobile repair. After decades of struggling to be a leader in all tire lines, Firestone has conceded that it is not always possible to do everything better than the competitors. The company's new philosophy reflects the fact that a major U.S. tire company does not have to manufacture what it wants to sell. Because of this point of view, the company has sold its huge heavy-duty radial truck tire facility to Japan's Bridgestone Tire, which has agreed to provide for Firestone's other production needs.

A CASE STUDY: THE RETURN OF SWISS WATCHMAKERS

The problems faced by Swiss watchmakers and how such problems were dealt with serve as a good illustration of how to adjust marketing strategies to cope with the IPLC. The Swiss were the first to invent the cuckoo clock and later, quartz technology. Unfortunately, Swiss firms viewed the quartz process as a specialty product with limited demand and remained with mechanical watches, which were less accurate. This misjudgment allowed such Japanese brands as Seiko and Citizen to swiftly and effectively penetrate the market with electronic models. The mistake was so costly that the Swiss watchmaking industry's share of the world market of 34 percent in the 1970s was halved a decade later. Many Swiss watchmakers were also nearly bankrupt.

Swiss watchmaking firms decided to make extensive adjustments to regain market share.[5] In terms of product policy, the Swiss made a commitment to production modernization. They were willing and prepared to make heavy investments in retooling. Furthermore, the manufacturing of most parts for expensive watch brands, previously scattered, was centralized at newly automated plants. Some 200 engineers, two years, and $8.5 million later, the number of watch parts being manufactured was cut in half to 51, allowing production costs to decline by more than 80 percent.

The Swiss watchmaking industry has also kept innovating. Longines, for example, introduced the VHP (very high precision) line, which had two quartz crystals instead of one. Swatch was another innovation. As a brightly colored watch, it was durable as well as fashionable. The later version of the Swatch intended to extend the product's life cycle was a fragrance model scented in mint, raspberry, and banana.

The Swiss industry has also segmented the market and offers product varieties for multiple market segments. It penetrated the mass market with Swatch. At the same time, while dominating the upper segment, the industry took aim at the upper-middle segment of the market, which had not yet been captured by Asian watchmakers.

Swiss watchmakers have become aggressive marketers. Their watches are no longer promoted on the basis of function alone but also include an emphasis on fashion. They have introduced slimmer, more sophisticated models with thinner movements which are promoted as stylish yet high-tech products. Realizing that Japan's strength was limited to the low-end and middle segments of the watch market because of its inability to match the prestige of Switzerland in watchmaking, Swiss firms made a conscientious effort to sell mystique. The success in cultivating their high-fashion image enabled the Swiss to maintain their domination of the high-end segment with their luxury watches made of precious metal and gems.

Swatch, short for Swiss watch, is a prime example of the Swiss watchmaking industry's new competitiveness. The Swatch, developed in 1982, utilized a technology and design created and pioneered in 1971 by Tissot and Astrolon. The technology made it possible to have the movement (quartz works) built into a plastic case which also served as the main plate. The crystal was sealed by laser, and the watch is waterproof and shockproof and cannot be repaired. The technology allowed for total automation and reduced production costs. As a result, Swatch watches can be priced at less than $30 for the inexpensive mass market.

Production technology alone does not explain the success of Swatch. The high-style promotion of Swatch was also crucial to its success. Swatch was promoted as a trendy item. Mass production, mass distribution, and mass promotion all came together in this case to make the product an outstanding success.

SOME CAVEATS

Much like many theories, the IPLC does not purport to explain the behavior of all products and/or countries. Some products satisfy universal needs, while other needs are more local (i.e., country- or area-specific) in nature. Those products which are in demand worldwide are more likely to conform to the characteristics described by the IPLC theory. In contrast, a product whose appeal is more limited may not conform to the description since the demand outside of the initiating country may be minimal.

Frequently, the availability of natural resources and agricultural products is determined by climate and location. As such, the production of such products is less dependent on technology. Therefore, manufactured products with substitutable factors of production are more likely to conform to IPLC particulars than are their agricultural counterparts.

Furthermore, it is necessary to distinguish products that are functional- or engineering-related from those that emphasize style and beauty. Functional products can be standardized from a physical standpoint and can thus be produced virtually everywhere. On the other hand, the psychological aspect of a product cannot be easily duplicated. Consumers may prefer the prestige of Gucci and Izod LaCoste even though these brands are not necessarily superior to many alternatives when compared on the basis of objective criteria. When counterfeit products appear, they are a sign that the psychological aspect associated with a product or brand is sufficiently strong to prevent full-scale product standardization.

There are other factors which can either lengthen or shorten the IPLC. Protectionist measures are one of these elements. For example, the creation of the 1968 voluntary restraint agreements on steel between the United States and West Germany and Japan forced imports to initially decline by 3–9 million net tons before rising again later. In 1984, the United States once again had to obtain five-year restraint agreements with Australia, Brazil, Japan, Korea, Mexico, South Africa, and Spain.

It is desirable that further research be conducted in order to identify the common characteristics of those products which offer empirical support and to distinguish such characteristics from those of other products that do not follow the behavior described by the IPLC. The role of technological intensity in encouraging or discouraging imitation also warrants some investigation.

CONCLUSION

The concept of the IPLC is not exactly new—it is probably as old as the domestic PLC concept. Economists in the area of international trade have long described the IPLC phenomenon based on the framework of comparative advertising, and they have also provided some empirical evidence in support of the IPIC theory.

In spite of its significant implications for the creation of marketing and trade policies, the IPLC has not received the widespread attention and discussion it deserves. One probable reason for this may be that only a few international marketing textbooks cover the topic and, even in such cases, the coverage is very limited. Another problem is a failure to go beyond the discussion of the economic aspect to include marketing implications. Once the broader implications of the theory are understood, multinational marketers should find the IPLC to be very relevant in the marketing of new products abroad.

Based on the IPLC theory, product imitation, product standardization, and price competition encourage consumers to be more price sensitive and less brand loyal. Generally, consumers see no reason to buy U.S. products if such items are more expensive without exhibiting some significant advantage over products made by LDCs.

As a result, in the final analysis, the initiating nation, having lost the technological edge to low-wage LDCS, shifts from being a net exporter of the product to a net importer, thus completing the cycle. The implication for the innovator is that the cycle should not be allowed to be completed if this can be achieved.

No company should believe that it can remain unaffected because of the patents it holds. It is only a matter of time before competitors turn up. The fast pace of product diffusion—locally and internationally—should make it clear that competition may arise very quickly and at any time. To the unprepared innovator, the unexpected arrival of competition can be deadly. Any attempt to protect itself through protectionism is shortsighted and hardly the answer. What is needed to be effective is competitiveness—not submissiveness.

U.S. firms should also anticipate competition. Japanese firms are not known for their innovative behavior but for their superior imitative habits. There is no reason why U.S. firms cannot practice the same by refining and improving existing technologies. Regardless of whether Japanese firms may have unfair advantages due to their government's support policies, the fact remains that Japanese firms are very skillful in utilizing the technologies developed by someone else. It is this particular skill that U.S. firms need to acquire.

For many basic industries, reversals should be anticipated. All may not be lost, however, since firms in such circumstances can still make appropriate adjustments in their marketing mix. For example, firms may want to eliminate those products which have no advantage and retreat into more defensible, well-defined segments. These firms can become specialists—not generalists—to battle in these carefully selected segments.

U.S. firms can anticipate reversal by observing the critical signs. Some of the indicators are: (1) a technological edge that is eroding or improvements that become more and more difficult, (2) LDCs being able to produce simple versions of the product, and (3) the product becoming standardized. The IPLC can be useful by pointing out the expected sequence of events, and it can exhort U.S. manufacturers to make timely and appropriate adjustments in marketing strategy.

NOTES

1. Alok K. Chakrabarti, Stephen Feinman, and William Fuentivilla, "A Cross-National Comparison of Patterns of Industrial Innovations," *Columbia Journal of World Business* 17 (Fall 1982): 33–39.

2. See Sak Onkvisit and John J. Shaw, "An Examination of the International Product Life Cycle and Its Application Within Marketing," *Columbia Journal of World Business* 18 (Fall 1983): 73–79.

3. Lloyd R. Kenward, "The Decline of the U.S. Steel Industry," *Finance & Development*, December 1987, pp. 30–33.

4. "Robots: Ours Are Smarter; Theirs Sell Better," *Chicago Fed Letter*, November 1987, pp. 1–3.

5. "The Real Story about the 'Swatch' Watch," *Jewelers' Circular-Keystone*, June 1985, pp. 54, 56; "A Last-Minute Comeback for Swiss Watchmakers," *Business Week*, 26 November 1984, pp. 139, 142.

Index

About the Authors

SAK ONKVISIT is Associate Professor of Marketing at San Jose State University.

JOHN J. SHAW is Associate Professor of Marketing at Providence College.